Rose Porter

In Quietness and in Confidence

A Heart to Heart Diary

Rose Porter

In Quietness and in Confidence
A Heart to Heart Diary

ISBN/EAN: 9783337191467

Printed in Europe, USA, Canada, Australia, Japan

Cover: Foto ©ninafisch / pixelio.de

More available books at **www.hansebooks.com**

A

HEART-TO-HEART DIARY.

By ROSE PORTER,

Author of "Honoria"; "In the Shadow of His Hand"; "A Year of Blessing"; Etc., Etc.

NEW YORK:
ANSON D. F. RANDOLPH & COMPANY,
38 WEST TWENTY-THIRD STREET.

TO

THE BLESSED MEMORY

OF

MY MOTHER:

WHOSE EARTHLY LIFE TAUGHT

"When He giveth quietness
Who then can make trouble?"

Remember,

"In quietness and in confidence shall be your strength."

Is. xxx. 15.

For,

"When He giveth quietness, who then can make afraid?"

Job xxxiv. 29.

"How beautiful within our souls to keep
This treasure the All-merciful hath given,
Grant it hearth and home.

. . . . .

Quiet where'er we roam,
Quiet around, within."

HYMNS OF THE AGES.

CONTENTS.

PRELUDE,	11
I.—IN QUIETNESS,	17
II.—THE CALL OF THE "STILL, SMALL VOICE," "COME,"	35
III.—THOUGHTS ON WORK,	53
IV.—RICH TOWARD GOD,	67
V.—BREAD UPON THE WATERS,	83
VI.—CHASTENING,	103
VII.—THE AGE WE LIVE IN,	117
VIII.—WILDERNESS DAYS,	135
IX.—DESERT PLACES,	157
X.—OPEN WINDOWS,	183

PRELUDE.

A HEART-TO-HEART diary! The thought of it came to me with the dawning of the New Year.

But, I am not sure that the word *diary* expresses my idea, for I have no plan for detailing emotions, or recording the subtle working of self-introspection, even though it be interwoven with aspiration.

No, self is the very thing I want to keep out of sight, for the intruding of self, in hours of quiet meditation, is like walking across a sandy plain when the sky is cloudless, and the sun at that point in the heavens which lets our shadow fall forward rather than backward.—And—who wants to walk with the shadow of self leading the way? "Self"—"that black spot in our sunshine," as Carlyle terms it.

Ah! Dear Lord, I pray Thee, henceforth let the shadow of self fall behind, not before; and it will, if the soul abides in the quietness the Lord giveth.

Yes, the quietness and confidence wherein is strength, like the "peace which passeth understanding," is God's gift, hence the preciousness of it, for the giver makes the value of the gift.

No wonder, then, this God-given quietness is deep and reposeful as the calm of a midsummer noon, the hour which enfolds nature in a tender silence that is like "a white hushed Presence."

And yet, though this "quietness and confidence" may be the soul's true environment, life, and its mystery, like wind among the tree-tops, is full of restless stirring. How to reconcile the one to the other is the problem that meets us on the threshold of these pages, and the practical question growing out of it is, How are we, you and I, dear H——, in the living of our daily lives, to adjust the relation of contemplation to action?

Is God brought near by action that we may contemplate Him, or is He brought near that we may be fitted to work for Him?

Old Philo the Jew maintained that "action must precede contemplative life in order that the latter be healthy." But, I think we can fix no rule, for surely God orders in our lives the way we must take to find Him, and our part is to follow that way whether it leads to active or passive service; and just as true is it that we must not let thoughts of action make us forget that "they also serve who stand and wait," as that we must not let meditation cripple our action. Acknowledging this, let our object in these ponderings on the soul's life be, then, the striving to find how we may enter into service through both, for we know God bids us render both, and our by-gone experiences have taught us, He can speak to us in the tumult of the storm, in the thronging rush of pressing duties, as well as in still, calm hours. Better, do you say, for "How can silence have a voice?"

We will take that question for our first "Heart-to-Heart" meditation, and come, let us listen, and hear "the silence open like a flower."

IN QUIETNESS.

"The love of God. . . . .
. . . . This is the peace of Heaven on earth. This is quiet."

"Sit still, my daughter."
RUTH iii. 18.

"Commune with your own heart, ... and be still. . . . . Put your trust in the Lord."
Ps. iv. 4, 5.

Remember,

"A quiet, patient heart that meekly serves the Lord, God's finger joys to touch, it is His harpsichord.

I.

IN QUIETNESS.

QUIETNESS of soul! This is one of those spiritual truths, that in its fulness can only be spiritually discerned, and can only be ours as we *live* it.

For in the matter of religious truth there is a difference, "the tree of knowledge is not necessarily the tree of Life." Life! living in, goes deeper than knowledge. Let us remember this, as we ponder the mystery of silence, of stillness before God, for only the living soul can hear the echoes of the Voice that fills

"Faith's ear with still delight."

Let us remember, too, a mind may be still though active, and that the quietness which is part of "the confidence" we have in Him, the Christ, is only found in the close abiding in Him, emblemed in His own parable of the Vine and the branch.

You must not lose heart because you do not come to know this nearness all at once, for love involves constant growth, and conformity to His will; hence the longer we follow that will, the more the soul, by God's grace, expands. Then, too, in our Shepherd's guiding, there are pastures and pastures, sheltered meadows where He gently leads, as well as high table-lands of verdure, up to which, as they become ready for mountain-top life, He carries His flock one by one, safe folded in His arms of Love.

There is something so close and personal in all this, a special tenderness for our individual need, that fills the soul with a sense of infinite quiet, for out of special tenderness grows special understanding, and the sweet, reposeful assurance that there is no massing of His sheep; each and every one is as much apart, filling a place all their own in God's sight, as the leaves on a tree are distinct one from the other.

Perhaps this is why the fullest communion we hold with our Lord is suggested by the type of "a still, small voice." You know how it is in our earthly lives, the words of love that are the dearest, and all for ourselves are the softly whispered ones, that we only hear. And, surely, the Lover of Souls, in keeping tryst with His chosen, in the same way comes nearest to us, when His words are for us alone, and,

"Truly in all eternity, no tone can be so sweet,
As when man's heart with God's in unison doth beat."

Grace, too, never seems so full, as when we recognize the personal element held in the promise, "My grace is sufficient for *thee*." Fears never melt away so swiftly as when we meet them in the safe encompassing of the assurances: "When *thou* passeth through the waters, I will be with thee." "My rod and my staff shall uphold *thee*." Service is never so dear and blessed a following of Christ, as when in response to His call, "Come unto me, all ye," we pass beyond the general invitation to the fellowship of the after words, "Take my yoke upon *you*, and learn of me."

Christ's yoke! What a close uniting of individual companionship that involves!——

Truly, so profound is the mystery of this

life hid in Christ, to each of His dear followers "the quietness and confidence wherein is strength," is only found in this *aloneness*, this oneness with Him, who knows our soul's deepest depth and need, for, "He made the spirit we are of."

If you realize all that is meant by this, you have come, dear H——, to a very "quiet resting-place." Repeat the words, "He made the spirit we are of," and with them link the verse from the Gospel according to St. John, "All things were made by Him, and without Him was not anything made that was made." By Him who came and lived on earth as the Man Christ Jesus— have you ever dwelt on the truth, that creation was the Function of the God Christ as well as salvation?

As I look from my window to-day, the whole world seems bathed in His love, glowing in the light of the life of Him whose peculiar office in the spiritual world is God revealing, and in the natural too, for Nature's chapter of revelation is hardly less full than the Spirit's, it is a page so wide spread of an ever open book clear writ to the seeing heart.

But let us turn from these thoughts, while with reverence we strive to learn the lessons taught by silence, strive to discover why by quietness of soul strength is obtained. And note that growth in strength is a sure outcome of silence in regard to our own sorrows, daily cares, perplexities, and annoyances.

I do not mean that silence which comes when the soul is shaken to its very foundation, and we are dumb, because the anguish is beyond words, but I mean that "stillness in God which is the perfect life, the grace of tranquillity." This is the quietness He means us to learn by and through sorrow, and by what a blessed rosary of comfort-laden promises He teaches us this lesson step by step. But, before we can take the first step, we must "put Him between one's self and one's grief"—and even then, as Harriet Monsell writes: "It will take a long time to learn, because one is slow to take in the stilling of self-acting that God may act in us, by His inner work." Nevertheless, she adds, "I am convinced this stillness, which is by no means inaction, *is* God's call to us as we advance in holiness."

Advance—I want you to heed that word, and remember it means, "He that believeth shall not make haste." Hence we see sure growth is wont to be slow growth. We may require to sow and sow again, and when at last the seeds of desire after holiness do take root, still there will be need for us to learn of nature, whose law is, first the bud, and then the unfolding, leaf by leaf, before the flower is a bloom, and more gradual even is the progress of ripening fruit.

What a sweet quieting of soul there is in all this—what a tender bidding of patient waiting for the "confidence" which holds "strength" for sorrowful hours. Patience! Yes—surely it is a blossom of which the root is quietness. "Be patient in tribulation"—"Possess your soul in patience"—thus the commands read, and patience implies quiet submission of heart before God's dealings.

But I repeat, it is slowly learned, and involves a sacrifice of *self*, quite, if not more complete than active service demands. And yet, as we apply this truth to the uncomplaining bearing of sorrow, how marvellously eloquent its very silence becomes, revealing to us that we must not expect light to illumine our darkness before we have discovered the blessing hidden in the darkness, for there is always a blessing linked with every sorrow. God grant us the faith to find it, for, as I said, it is surely there, an immortal hope, even though as the winding tissues enwrap the chrysalis, it may be for a time shut in with the darkness. The parable of "the leaven hid in three measures of meal" tells us this—and, knowing it is there, can we not be patient even if we have to wait till the whole is leavened? Darkness—and waiting—yes—they both have their own lesson, for spite the soul's sureness of the Everlasting Arms that support with an upholding clasp that only the sorrow-touched know, God sends the affliction, and He means sorrow to be sorrow, and to do its work, else where were the chastening of His Love? And if there were no darkness, how could we learn the *obedience* of faith?—the patient waiting for the "day to break when shadows flee away"?—

"They never can fly away," do you say, "till earth is exchanged for Heaven," for sorrow never leaves the heart into which it has really entered. In one sense you are right, and yet in another, I think you are wrong, in that statement, dear H——. I agree with you that real sorrow leaves a scar as long lasting as our mortal life, even though sometimes it does seem quickly and rudely pushed aside; still it stays, but natures are different, and in nothing do we see this difference more sharply defined than by the way griefs are met and borne. And, anyway, it is not our place to judge the seemingly shallow-hearted, but without judging we know in earnest natures, as time goes on, and some seem to forget sorrow, it is only *seeming*, and from the fact, too, that it has become inwrought as a part of self, hence it no longer stands out in the bold relief of a separate thing.

And if sometimes this makes us more lonely, because we feel the lack of the sympathy with which at first friends encompassed our every hour, this very feeling is a pasture place, for there is a precious side to this craving for human sympathy, because in it our Lord meets us very closely, for when on earth He, too, felt it.

Do you remember how He told His disciples "the Son of Man must suffer many things"? Were not those words a plea for sympathy? And then, how He bade them "watch with Him one hour," thus again repeating the same desire. And yet, how they failed Him! for His sorrow was to them as an unread page, and the servant is not above his Master.

In hours of great loneliness, and when you feel you are not fully understood, it will help you to follow this thought, for even if it lead "into the cloud" you will know *He* entered that cloud before you, and He knows all about the trial of loneliness—all about it!

But as you thus think, never fail to remember, whatever the weight of Christ's anguish, His heart was always open to the needs of others; and if we follow Him, we, too, must keep open eyes, and open hearts for the burdens those about us may be called to carry, and that perhaps our sympathy can make less heavy.

This is one of the places I almost fear to approach, for there is always danger of making a mistake in the manner of offering sympathy, and I hesitate in giving even a suggestion as to "the best way." One thing certainly it is well to remember, and that is, that grief is as truly a *possession* as anything else, hence the feeling of warm pity for others gives us no right to handle and touch the wounded place with any claim to dictate or control.

Do you recall how Bunsen wrote, "A man has nothing more sacred, of all that is essentially his own, than his grief." All this makes quiet sympathy the safest, and almost always it is the most acceptable.

And if by dividing miles we be too far separated from the sorrowing friends we love, to whisper, "My dear!"—"my dear!"—one cannot go far amiss by sending the simple words, "Remember God loves—and God knows." And in truth, when hearts are crushed, this is about all they can take in.

I trust I am right in telling you this. I think the really sorrowful will say, "Yes, the sweetest of all solace is quiet sympathy." Surely, it is the flower of self-forgetfulness, that blossoms out of still communion with Him who alone can give wisdom for the blessed ministry of consolation. A ministry that is bounded on every side by the command, "Let the same mind be in you that was in Christ Jesus."

The having that mind will solve, too, our own perplexities, as to how we ourselves are to meet trials in the childlike spirit of quiet submission that clings with a child's confidence to the strength of Him who "doth not afflict willingly," but for the sake of the ripening of the "afterward peaceable fruits of righteousness."

I need hardly tell you the sorrows to which I have alluded are the deepest griefs that human hearts can know. For the comforting of lesser trials by sympathy I would not so strictly enjoin silence—for to some natures, "little troubles," when spoken out, vanish like mist before sunshine; nevertheless, in speaking of one's own special trials, I do think we grow stronger when we accept them silently, knowing "the Infinite Hand behind the clouds gives only the sorrows we can bear," and remembering if He multiplies them, "they who suffer much, are like those who know many languages, they are learning to understand and be understood by all."

There is another truth which I need hardly tell you, and yet I would not have you pass it by. It is, that the peace and repose of possessing a mind quiet like our Lord's is purely spiritual, and not according to the world's interpretation of quietness. For this inner calmness of soul is something all outside of circumstances, and it is the something which makes "the cross of Christ the pledge to us, that even the deepest suffering may be the condition of the highest blessing."

This is one of those complex truths that are much like some musicful symphony, where the "rest" in the strain is the part which most clearly brings out the underlying harmony that like a golden thread runs through bass and treble, linking lower, higher, and midway notes in one complete whole, and it is a true type of the quiet "pause-places" that come in the midst of these lives of ours. Places where the still, small voice reveals to the listening soul that "secret of the Lord" which is the chain that links our struggles *here* with victory *there*. A secret which we know is in safe keeping even when the waves of life's tossing oceans are most turbulent, and well-nigh deafen our power of listening to that whispering Voice. Yet we know it is safe, I repeat, for "He is willing and able to keep that which we have committed to Him."

Thinking of it thus, it seems much as it does when, on a summer morning, we look across some wide stretch of sea-water toward the horizon line, which is hardly visible, so heavy hangs the misty veil that is waiting for the sun to rise and scatter its cloud-like vapor, and yet we know, it is all that divides us from a clear sight of the up-hill slope of the sky that leads to the rounded vault of Heaven's blue dome. Try to remember this "emblem of the sky" when next the brooding clouds of trial come like a vapor between your soul and the Heaven-ward path, that like altar-stairs leads the heart of faith *Up* to the Heart of Love.

And now I have filled my paper so full, scarce space enough is left for me to bid you strive to meet daily cares, perplexities, and annoyances with all the quietness you can cull from God's promised help, which is your confidence and strength; but it is just as well, for no one can make a rule for another's conduct in matters of the soul's life. The being true to your own conviction of right, being in profound earnest, and the humbly asking how Christ would have acted under the same circumstances, is all the guide I could give you were I to write pages, so I will only add the "Rosary" of Bible verses I promised, for they all point toward the acquirement of spiritual strength, through spiritual quietness.

A ROSARY OF SILENCE.

"Be silent before the Lord . . . for, lo, I come, and I will dwell in the midst of thee, saith the Lord" (Zech. ii. 10, 19).

"Take heed, and be quiet; fear not, neither be faint-hearted" (Is. vii. 4).

"The work of righteousness shall be peace: and the effect of righteousness, quietness and assurance forever" (Is. xxxii. 17).

"And my people shall dwell in a peaceable habitation, and in sure dwellings, and in quiet resting places" (Is. xxxii. 18).

"The word of the Lord came to me, saying . . . . I will give peace and quietness; . . . . be strong, and of good courage; dread not, nor be discouraged" (1 Ch. xxi. 9, 13).

"For when He giveth quietness, who then can make afraid?" (Job xxxiv. 29).

"Whoso hearkeneth unto me shall dwell safely, and shall be quiet from fear of evil" (Prov. i. 33).

"It is a good thing that a man should both hope and quietly wait for the salvation of the Lord" (Lam. iii. 26).

"Thine eyes shall see a quiet habitation" (Is. xxxiii. 20).

"And better is a handful with quietness, than both the hands full with vexation of spirit" (Eccl. iv. 5).

> "Quiet, Lord, my froward heart;
>   Make me teachable and mild,
> Upright, simple, free from art;
>   Make me as a little child:
> From distrust and envy free,
> Pleased with all that pleases Thee.
>
> "What Thou shalt to-day provide,
>   Let me as a child receive;
> What to-morrow may betide,
>   Calmly to Thy wisdom leave:
> 'Tis enough that Thou wilt care,
> Why should I the burden bear?
>
> "As a little child relies
>   On a care beyond his own,
> Knows he's neither strong nor wise,
>   Fears to stir a step alone:
> Let me thus with Thee abide,
> As my Father, guard, and guide."

THE CALL OF THE "STILL, SMALL VOICE," "COME."

"Come thou, and all thine house, into the ark."
GENESIS viii. 1.

"O Lord and Master of us all,
 Whate'er our name or sign,
We own Thy sway, we hear Thy call,
 We test our lives by Thine."
WHITTIER.

"A holy thought is a 'Still, small Voice.'"

II.

THE CALL OF THE "STILL, SMALL VOICE," "COME."

HAVE you ever thought of the personality of the word *house*, or temple when it is used in the Bible to express the soul?

"Come thou, and all thine house, into the ark." Read that verse in the knowledge of God that shines in the faith of Jesus Christ, and tell me, do you not find it glowing with the warmth of a personal invitation?

In the faith of Jesus Christ! How true it is, in that radiance, God's word becomes "A lamp unto our feet, a light unto our path," for, the oil that feeds faith's lamp is Love. I am glad for to-day's meditation, the first word on which its beams fall is the blessed word "Come."

"Come,"—I think we never read it in the language of Holy Scripture without seeming to see the Hand extended in welcome, without seeming to hear the Voice, unlike any other voice, "still and small," whispering—"Come"—"Come unto me."

"Come,"—God grant it may be our portal word leading within to the mystery of the "inner life," for the life of the soul is a mystery.

"Inner life."—Do you ask what it is? The answer is not far to seek: "In Christ," holds the reply.

Ah, the comfort of this nearness of companionship with our Lord,—thank God, it is implanted in the New Testament as a foundation principle of discipleship as firmly as "the mountains are round about Jerusalem."

Yes, whatever our outward life may be,—and we must know an outer life, else how could we learn to be "*in* the world, yet not *of* it," — always we have this "ark of strength, our resting and our hiding place in Christ."

But remember, only as we obey His call, and Come, can we know the quietness of soul that belongs to abiding in His Presence. A quietness that is like the sweet mellow silence of some still wood, that holy calm of spirit that is akin to the unfathomable azure of the deep sky.

Do you tell me, dear H——, all this is easy to write, and yet it holds no clear answer to your question—"How can *I* come?" True enough, nevertheless that is one of those questions whose answer is only found in coming. "He that believeth hath the witness in himself." Your part is to test belief by its effects; I can do no more than assure you it will be "peace and quietness."

Still I will give you a line from Tennyson which helped me once when perplexed as you are now,

> "I cannot understand, I love."

Do you find in it a hint broad enough to serve for a reply? Note, it bids you love, and if you love, sure am I you will come, and coming, dark places will grow light, even light enough for you to learn,

> "Through all the future of thy years,
> To form thy life in likeness of thy Lord's."

And now let us turn again to the emblem thought that pictures the soul under the metaphor of a house or temple. It guides by a straight pathway from the Old, on, to the New Testament; and yet like all the paths of the Lord, there are many halting places by the way, where the weary may rest by the "brook of the willows" (Isa. xv. 7), or in "groves by the green trees upon the high hills" (Jer. xvii.). But we will only pause to record the Prophet's command to the dying king, "Set thine *house*—thy soul—in order," and Solomon's assurance that "wisdom hath builded her *house*, she hath hewn out her seven pillars."

What are the soul's seven pillars of wisdom? Verily, in seeking a reply there is need for us to pray,

"O Lord of Hosts, all Heaven possessing,
Reveal to us each secret meaning of all Thy Word's divinest lore."

Open our eyes that we may see, our ears that we may hear.

Seven pillars!—Are they strong staffs for the uplifting and supporting of the heavy-laden branches on which grow the "fruits of the Spirit"? Do they hold up toward the Sun of Righteousness those fruits that can know no ripening save as the Heavenly beams nourish and perfect their growth?

This is the interpretation we will take, and let us link to it St. Paul's definition of those special "spiritual fruits." I am so glad he gave them each a name and meaning all their own, making them stand out well-nigh as vividly as the Blessings which gem our Saviour's mountain sermon. And following Paul's guidance, and taking Christ Jesus for the chief "corner-stone" of all our efforts after up-building, let us by way of help in the worthily living these daily lives of ours, plant the spiritual fruits around the seven pillars of wisdom, which God grant may already be set firm in our souls.

First of all is "*Love*"; for love twines about the pillar that is nearest the "Corner-stone." We know this, for its superscription tells us: "He who loveth God, loveth his brother also." And "he that loveth shall be loved of my Father, and I will love him" (John xiv. 21).

Love, too, is the fruit which secures all the others, for he who loves, trusts. And think what a foremost place love fills in the Gospel record,

> "Think well how Jesus trusts Himself
> Unto our love." . . .

And

> "His love of us may teach us how
> To love Him in return :
> Love cannot help but grow more free
> The more its transports burn."

"*Joy*" is the next fruit in Paul's enumeration—Joy, Holy Joy. It is a slow growth in the Christian's soul; it is hard to learn, for the joy of which Paul tells is the "rejoicing in tribulation."

"How can we thus rejoice?" Because of the *afterward*, dear H——. Afterward! I hardly know a word fuller of comfort for God's children than that, and yet there are so many comfort-laden words—so many!

"*Peace*."—Our Saviour Himself tells us its support. Such a strong pillar, even His promise, "Peace I leave with you, my peace I give unto you." Never forget this peace which passeth understanding is Christ's gift! Peace—it is well it foreruns "*Long-suffering*." Surely Paul knew we would need the one to help us meet the other. Hence he ranked them as he did.

Suffering! How to define it I am powerless, it comes in ways so manifold; and truly each "heart knoweth its own bitterness." And yet suffering is a wonderful revealer. It speaks an open language to those who have the "key of love," even while at the same time it is a pillar in the soul hung heavy with mystery.

But one thing is very plain, and that is, the *blessing* of sorrow does *not* consist in the suffering it brings. No, "it consists in the spiritual response to suffering of one whose confidence in the Supreme Source of Love and Goodness cannot be thus overcome; it consists in the angels of Peace that came to strengthen Christ when He was *willing* to drink the cup that God might glorify His own name."

What a tender manifestation of Christ's care for us, His followers, we find in His anticipation that the enigma of permitted suffering was a question that would echo on as long as time lasts, and thus He set for its quieting the same seal to its *why* that He applied as a test to His own willingness to endure, even the glory of God.

Do you remember it is written, "And His disciples asked Him, saying, Master, who did sin, this man or his parents, that he was born blind? Jesus answered, Neither hath this man sinned, nor his parents, *but that the works of God should be* made manifest in him."—"Now a certain man was sick, named Lazarus. Then his sisters sent unto Him, saying, Lord, behold, he whom thou lovest is sick. When Jesus heard that, He said, This sickness is not unto death, *but for the glory of God*, that the Son of God might be *glorified thereby.*"——

I am so thankful for this "trailing cloud of glory" that illumes our darkness, and that nowhere in the Bible can we find that God or Christ demands that suffering is to be accepted or sought for its own sake; so thankful there is no such narrow limit as that to the chastening which makes part of Christ's call, bidding us "come" to Him.

We know, too, the pillar that upholds sorrow, and that is planted deep in every human soul, is both a rod and a staff in one. It is this knowledge that gives us strength to ask that we may enter into "the fellowship of His suffering."

It is a profoundly solemn petition to offer. Think! it means to "be conformed to His death," that is, to be made like Him. Ah! if we can thus pray, even though the soul's path heavenward leads "up-hill all the way," we are well nigh the summit, I think; we begin

> "To feel from burdening cares and ills,
> The strong uplifting of the hills,"

even the everlasting hills from "whence cometh help."

But this is one of the places, where in pondering on the "Man of Sorrows," and what it means to follow His steps, we need to tread very carefully lest we make a mistake.

For, "while sorrows, disappointments were around Christ, moulding Him on all sides, the element in which His strength was made, His life lived; yet love, faith, hope, the joy of the soul in God, were the inspirations from which they came, and to which they rose." And they gave Him power to become "acquainted with grief," but at the same time to behold its other, its *on*ward side.

Then, too, "He who was made perfect by suffering, never could succumb to suffering, nor permit the sense of it to be dominant in His nature," for while self-sacrifice must involve pain, yet, as Phillips Brooks expresses it, "He carried the song and the trumpet always in His heart. That life, marking its way with drops of blood, on which the pity of the world has dwelt more tenderly than over any other life it knows, has yet always seemed to the world's best standards to be a true triumphal march, radiant with splendor all along the way, and closing in a true victory at last." And, to continue the quotation, "One of the brightest insights which we ever get into the human heart and its essential breadth and justice, and its power, when it is working at its best, to hold what seem contradictory ideas in their true spiritual harmony, is given to us when we see how men have been able to see together both sides of the life of Jesus, to pity His sorrow and to glory in His happiness, and yet to blend both of these two thoughts of Him into one single idea of one single self-consistent Christ. It is a sort of witness of how truly men, in that highest mood into which they are drawn when they try to study Christ, easily see the real truth with regard to human life, which is that in it joy and pain, so far from being inconsistent with and contradictory to one another, are, in some true sense, each other's complement, and neither alone, but both together, make the true sum of human life."

Pause a moment here, to note the deep and tender significance of the way in which our Lord met the most suffering hours of His life. How marked is the truth that "He never let suffering give the direction to His feelings nor suggest His thoughts."

This is a very full example for us to contemplate, and that you may quite clearly see its meaning, I copy the words of an English writer, for they make it very plain: "When He is departing from the temple for the last time, the Rejected forever, He sees the widow with her mite, the beauty of the offering takes possession of His heart, and instead of mourning for Himself, He is blessing *her*. At the last supper no word of sorrow is breathed by *Him*, no fear but for the imperfect fidelity of those whom on the morrow He was to leave to their own strength, whilst the sorrow of the disciples is gently reproved as far from the occasion:

Let not your hearts be troubled, ye believe in God, believe also in me.' 'Peace I leave with you, my peace I give unto you.' 'If ye loved me ye would rejoice, because I go to my Father.' Whilst bearing His own cross, there is solicitude for others, but peace for Himself: 'Women of Jerusalem, weep not for me; weep for yourselves and for your children.' And on the cross itself all suffering leads to the suggestions of mercy, the prayer of forgiveness, the last directions to love, the consciousness of being perfectly safe in the hands of God. When, then, we call Christ 'the Man of Sorrows,' let us remember what we mean; that He was one whose spiritual nature suffering never ruled, whose peace, hope, and love sorrow could perfect, but could not disturb. .... He passed through the fulness of sorrow as He passed through the fulness of temptation, and had the brightness of His spiritual love dimmed by neither."

If we enter into the heart of this, dear H——, how it broadens our prayer that we may have "fellowship with Him," for such fellowship would cause us to meet our life, even though it be sorrow-encompassed, with cheerful energy, in a brave, trustful spirit, ready to turn from our own griefs with hearts of love and self-forgetfulness, reaching out in help toward others, and finding pleasure in self-sacrifice.

And yet, despite this, sometimes the clouds hang low, and though the mountain heights are shining, we are down in the valley, and our eyes seem holden when we seek to scan their topmost summits.

Well!—there is one thing we can always do at such times, and perhaps this is why they come to us; we can trust in love when we cannot see, for it does not need sight to hold on, knowing

> " Forever from the Hand that takes
>   One blessing from us others fall ;
> And, soon or late, our Father makes
>   His perfect recompense to all !"

This truth I am sure we can learn from the fruits of "*Goodness*" and "*Gentleness*" that clasp their tendrils so firmly around wisdom's pillars. And now comes "*Faith*," for we have gone the round. Faith leads us back to Love, just as Love leads us on to Faith. And the corner-stone, in which both are firm set, holds the chain that links the one with the other; while like the hinges of a strong gateway before Faith and Love, the entrance swings wide open, and we are safe " in Christ," "in whom all the building fitly framed together groweth into an holy *temple* in the Lord," "an habitation of God through the Spirit."

So we come again to the opening thought of our meditation, the *home* of which our soul stands as a type. Our Saviour Himself tells us this, for "He spoke of the temple of His body,"—the body in one sense signifying that self-hood which in the days of our mortal life is so a part, as it were, in its subtle interblending and working with what we call the soul, that both are needful to bring out the full idea of either, for they are dependent one on the other for the accomplishment of any active or tangible work, as much as root and branch are both needed to make a tree. Hence the metaphor, " The earthly house of this tabernacle, which is the temple of the living God." And "the temple of God is holy." Can we add the afterpart of the verse, "which temple ye are"? With humble reverence I think we may, for

True life grows on from small to great,
Each year, each day, its increase finds;
Nor is it the " blind force " of fate,
That earthly sorrow ofttime blends,
With the pure work of grace, the more to consecrate
The love which ever in its sacred yearning heaven-
    ward tends.

Are you weary? Have patience a little longer, for I cannot leave the call that bids us enter within the ark of safety and quiet, without lingering a moment to ponder the *fulness* of the invitation.

It reads, not only, "come thou," but "*all thine house.*"—*All.* It is a brief word, yet broad enough to compass our every need, for there is nothing too great, nothing too small for us to bring to the One of all compassion. *All* may come into the ark. Yes, it is true God is so great that there is with Him no small and no great things. Such distinctions fade before the Power that can give *all things.*

When we really feel this, the place prayer fills in the soul so widens; it becomes like those trees which unfold new leaves even while the old remain, for the echo of one prayer does not die away before another begins. And—I think it is the going to God with our every want that He loves. Hence the oftener we go, the more we please Him, for our asking for the, to us, seemingly little things is but demonstrating our entire dependence on Him, and surely this dependence, this trust, is what makes us the *children* of our Heavenly Father.

It is the essence of that "perfect love which casteth out fear," and when it takes possession of the soul, even though for long years we may stay here on earth, our spirits live in the presence of the Unseen, for "it is the soul that sees," and

" He who sees the Future, sure
The baffling Present may endure,
And bless meanwhile the Hand that leads
The heart's desires beyond the halting steps of deeds."

Enter the ark, then, "fear not"; bring your *all* things; your temptations, your doubts, your sorrows, and your joys, your efforts and your failures; bring them *all* to Him who bids you "Come."

" Who would not go,
With bouyant steps to gain that blessed portal,
Which opens to the land we want to know,
Where shall be satisfied the souls immortal.
Who would not go ? "

THOUGHTS ON WORK.

"Every place that the sole of your feet shall tread on, that have I given you." JOSHUA i. 3.

"Is it hard to serve God, timid soul? Hast thou found
   Gloomy forests, dark glens, mountain-tops on thy way?
All the hard would be easy, all the tangles unwound,
   Wouldst thou only desire, as well as obey."
FABER.

III.

THOUGHTS ON WORK.

REMEMBER it is one thing to know God's gifts, another thing to accept them. And while it is true that God has given us a land of promise in Christ, it yet remains for us to take possession of it; we must set "the sole of our feet" upon it for ourselves. To-day let us apply this truth to work, in whose domain it holds firm sway, for while every task God gives us contains a blessing, yet we must find that blessing for ourselves.

But you say—"We cannot find it, save as God reveals it to us." Your words, dear H——, lead to one of the mystery places that only grows plain to the heart in which faith rules—one of the places where the soul's altar is inscribed, "Lord, I believe,— help Thou mine unbelief."

St. Paul states this complex truth in the

verse, "Work *out* your own salvation, for it is God who worketh *in* you," hence we see, like all the experiences of spiritual life, it involves a joint work. There is no such thing as aloneness when once we have accepted God's will as our will, and no sooner do we perceive this, than we also see it is the Holy Spirit that wakens aspiration in our souls. Yes, we know all earnest impulse, all desire after good comes from the "Spirit," while our part is the weaving impulse into steady purpose, desire into fruitful deed; and how the recognition of this sanctifies our daily life, how it enfolds us very near to God. Let us strive to remember this, and that when a lofty aspiration, a tender thought, a great yearning to help others comes flooding the soul with Heavenly radiance, lighting up even the common "every-dayness" of life with glory, it is God "*working in us*," scattering in the garden of our hearts the holy seeds of desire for service, for Christ's sake; and, remember also that only as we faithfully tend and nourish them will they grow and bear flower and fruit; only thus will we come at last to know what the "Harvest-Home-

Song" means, for only to believers are songs of everlasting joy promised, and workers are believers.

But we must be patient, we must not expect the harvest straightway to follow the planting. Nature teaches us this, for as in the natural so in the spiritual, "the blade is not the full corn"; but, though it may be well-nigh imperceptible, growth is sure, if the laws of growth are heeded. In the soul's life you know the chief law, keep close to the source of growth, close to Him who has promised to be as "the dew unto Israel," and that "there shall be an handful of corn in the earth, upon the top of the mountains; the fruit thereof shall shake like Lebanon." What a meaningful verse this is!—only a handful of corn, and yet, because planted by faith, on the mountain-top, close up, near to God, right under the very sunlight as it were of His Presence, its fruit becomes of value sufficient to be numbered under the wide-spreading metaphor of Lebanon. "Cast forth his roots as Lebanon." What a promise that for workers in the Lord's vineyard! And then comes, "His branches shall spread, His beauty shall be as the olive-tree, and His smell as Lebanon." How fragrant a type this of the healing odor of the cedar, which is so beautiful an emblem of service and steady growth upward, fuller to me of suggestion than any other of the Bible-named trees of which it is written, "Break forth into singing, O forest, and every tree therein, for the Lord hath redeemed Jacob." .... "All the trees of the forest shall clap their hands,"—"the trees of the wood shall rejoice at the presence of the Lord." No wonder trees and their language are so voiceful, when every breeze is thus a whispered "Praise the Lord," every stirring of the branches a repetition of "O ye winds of God, bless ye the Lord: praise Him, and magnify Him forever."—"Even the dead leaves at our feet, and the skeleton trees above us, give us a sort of infant school lesson in human history, teaching us to spell some syllables of the promise of being once more clothed upon"—thus Caroline Fox writes, and she adds: "And what shall we make of the evergreens? I think I know human evergreens too, whose change is but a translation."

To return to the emblem thought—How full it is of blessing for those of whom the Lord said, "I will heal .... I will love freely," for we know it is His love, that gives us the power of loving, as well as the power to "grow as the vine, the scent thereof as the wine of Lebanon." What a full type, I repeat, this is of Christian service; how it pictures the liberal soul that in its giving out-reaches the narrow limit of self, and selfishness; and of the tender heart too, that goes forth on gentle errands of mercy for the comforting and the healing of the sorrowful and suffering, with a sweetness of deed that is like the fragrant penetrating of the reviving balsam, and strength-giving as the "wine of Lebanon."

I will not call these thoughts a wandering from our subject, for they all echo with hints of service. And now, I am wondering, will you assent to the words I chose as an index for our meditations to group about as we ponder work. I quote them from one who had tested their truth not merely by theory, but by the crucial test of daily experience.

"I believe," thus he says, "that the noblest discipline which life affords, is the daily wear and tear of petty annoyances, the little discomforts, pains, and burdens of ordinary life; thus the best work for Heaven is done in the home." If we agree to this, then we believe that all God sends to each human soul must have a sacred meaning, however trivial it may seem to our dim-eyed seeing. With what a glory that belief illumines life, making even the dullest task glow with a brightness, brighter than any light that ever yet shone on land or sea.

But, alas, seldom do we mount high enough to look beyond the mist of the present; seldom do we realize *work* is a consecrated thing. And yet, the divine consecration of labor is just as real a transmuting power now, as when first it laid its touch on the humble work of the humble Nazareth workshop. Now, as then, it can fit the bits of what we call "daily drudgery" into jewel places in the life patterns God has given us each to "work out." Patterns all so different, for no two lives are alike, and yet, spite this endless variety, the object of all life is the same, for God would have us all "conformed to the image of Christ."

Do you ask, "When the aim is one, why are the ways leading to its accomplishment so varied?"

Like many another question, we do not find the answer till we have followed Christ for long, for our love for Him is like all true love, a thing of progress, and the longer we follow, the longer we love, the more we understand, and yet He leads Christians who are far on only by a step at a time.

And the answering of our questions, the ever repeating "why," like our times of service, have their seasons for fruit. It is not ours to choose when these seasons come, but it is ours to *do* His will: ours to keep ever on the watch, ready to follow His bidding, even if it be naught more than the being "faithful in that which is least," remembering that least leads on to the "faithful in much."

You tell me that you admit all this, nevertheless it still perplexes you, that so much time is spent in doing things that do not any of them seem really worth doing.

I know one often feels so, and yet, if there is a "must be" in the tasks, we need not trouble as to their worth, however little they may seem, judged by a merely human estimate of value. This is one of the lessons we are to learn from the widow with her "two mites," and from the woman's bringing the weary Prophet "the little cake." So your perplexity is no new difficulty; earnest souls, eager after service for Christ's sake, have stumbled over it, ever since souls first began to seek to be "rich toward God." I know all about it, for many an hour I, too, have spent in that valley of shadows, and I hear the very sigh in your voice as you ask: "What is the use of this daily repetition of duties?"

I might fill a page with answers to that question, but I will linger to note only "one use" that helps me most in meeting and accomplishing what you call "dull, material work." It is, the asking my heart: May not these very things, that I find so irksome, from their seeming unimportance, hold the very opportunity my soul needs for the learning of what it means to submit my will to God's?——And, anything which helps toward *that* never can be called useless. In God's sight, the spirit in which we serve is so much more than the service. And is there not a solemn purpose in the very fact, that the duties—most of them—we are called to perform are little tasks? Are we not, even the very best of us, in danger of dwelling on what *we do*, rather than what *we are;* and nothing helps to keep us lowly in heart like the small self-denials, for what is more humbling than the finding even they cost an effort—while nothing reveals our innate pride of heart more surely than our ready willingness for great duties, our slow lagging over the lowly and commonplace.

Yes, it is true, to the demands of the high occasion for service, we rise like birds winging an upward flight, but to meet the humdrum everyday occasions with the eagerness and courage of a cheerful doer—Ah! that is not so easy.

In truth, there is only one way by which we can meet them thus, and that is, by remembering God made us as we are: He linked mind with body, the material with the spiritual, and we must take care of the one for the sake of the other, even if it does involve a somewhat tiresome doing "over and over" of daily duties, for they are duties. And, surely, we can trust God to make us all spirit, when we have learned the Heaven-preparing lesson of "little things," and no longer need the discipline of the body.

Let us strive, then, to go on bravely, for if we do we will find even "the plainest path of duty" admits of the "stamping daily things with beauty."

Another thought comes to me just here, that will, I think, prove helpful to us both. It is, that these "daily duties," like the husks which encircle the full-eared corn, have in them issues that reach far beyond the seen, even on to the "unseen and eternal." We are slow learners, we scholars in God's school, and many a tender leading, many an unfolding of His guidance is often required before we come to know this; often much of disappointment and suffering is needed, too, but when at last we do catch a glimpse of the truth that life's incompleteness here is but the prelude to completeness *there*, then every hour, and every task that fills it, becomes part of the *oneness*, the vast *whole* toward which our souls expand and reach out, as flowers reach out toward sunshine.

In the light of this blessed Hope, which tells of the illimitable Future, how even now, while our horizon is bounded by the limitations of the present, we yet begin to know something of the glory of our Hereafter; for though dwellers on earth, we are heirs of Heaven, "joint heirs with Christ." And—How near earth is to Heaven! So near!—for

> "Upward steals the life of man,
> As the sunshine from the wall:
> From the wall into the sky:
> From the roof along the spire.
> Ah! the souls of those that die
> Are but sunbeams lifted higher."

I have strayed from your perplexity regarding "useless work," a complaint, I think, you will never make again, now that we have seen even the most homely toil is stamped with the royal seal, "Do all in the name of our Lord Jesus Christ."

Every act, then, consecrate as "unto Him." Let *that* be the keynote of service, and obedience will be its harmony.

And, though the learning of simple childlike obedience may be a hard lesson, we know that the habit of obedience *here* is worth all it costs to acquire, since it will fit us for future service there. For

> "Time and obedience are enough,
> And thou a saint shall be."

RICH TOWARD GOD.

"Rich toward God."
LUKE xii. 21.

"We share in what is infinite ; 'tis ours,
  For we and it alike are Thine."
FABER.

IV.

RICH TOWARD GOD.

"RICH toward God!" I used those words as we pondered work, and ever since they have been knocking at the door of my heart, as though asking what I meant by them.

You remember the Gospel chapter, Luke 12th, in which they are recorded, and where they fill a mid-way place among a group of parables that all have to do with the deep things of the Spirit. For, if you will but study that chapter, dear H——, verse by verse, you will find many an unexpected lesson enfolded with its simplest teachings, reminding one of the flowers we find in spring among the grass-blades of a sunny meadow.

Teachings that are, too, like a succession of vivid panoramic portrayals of the underlying foundation truth, that "a man's life consisteth not in the abundance of the things which he possesseth." As our Saviour gave utterance to this sequel, as it were, to the "Sermon on the Mount," the fact that there were "gathered together" an "innumerable multitude of people," straightway makes plain why He impressed the lessons He taught by a series of simple metaphors, all suggested by objects and pursuits with which even the most unlearned among His hearers were familiar.

It explains, too, the why of contrasts sharply defined as darkness and light, a hidden-away closet and an open house-top, and also the emblem of birds, commonest of all the winged tribes, sparrows, five sold for two farthings!—But these teachings were hardly more than outline lessons, while in fuller detail glows the parable out of which we cull the necessity of being "rich toward God."

It is a wonderfully life-like picture, spite the eighteen centuries that divide now from then. We see it all as distinctly as we see some bold head-land that rises up out of well-nigh encircling sea-waves.

The portly, rich man, looking on his broad

fields that had brought forth so plentifully, planning the pulling down of the already ample barns that still greater may be made ready for the ingathering of the "goods that are to be laid up for many years." And then—how the picture changes—a shadow falls over the fair scene of earthly prosperity, as though it were born out of the very sunshine of the man's security, in the wealth of that ripened harvest. And in the brief compass of four lines we are taught the powerlessness of worldly possessions to secure worldly permanence, by a flash of truth that like some lamp in a lighthouse tower, has ever since shown a warning beam, lighting up the words, "*So* is he that layeth up treasures for himself and is not rich toward God." The value of all this for you and me, dear H——, is that it brings us to the question: "How can we attain the spiritual grace of being rich toward God?" And the reply is just the reverse of the world's way of estimating riches—Christ Himself gives us the answer, saying, "Learn of Me, for I am meek and lowly of heart."

Lowliness of heart combined with high effort and earnest struggle for success, truly the one seems opposed to the other, and according to our human-heart interpretation they are; but in Christ they become reconciled, for "in Him" we find the deep harmony of truth, and learn how humility and aspiration, the knowledge of the soul's sinfulness, and the knowledge of its boundless capacities, can walk hand in hand the path of this earthly pilgrimage, because "God's answer to man's constant aspiration heavenward, the impersonated bond between God and man is a 'Mediator,' as Scripture terms it, who bridges over the chasm which sin has opened between earth and Heaven." Bridges, too, over all the seeming contradictions which only exist because our understanding is clogged by earthly trammels, and hence we will need to open our souls wide to take in what it means, to have a heart so truly lowly that it is rich toward God. But before we ponder this, let us linger for a while amid the lessons of the grass-blades, and the lilies, and the birds which have neither storehouse nor barn, and yet God feedeth them, and :

> "It was not a poet's dream,
> An idle vaunt of song.

· · · · ·

"Which bids us see in heaven and earth,
    In all fair things around,
Strong yearnings for a blest new birth
    With sinless glories crowned!

"Which bids us hear at each sweet pause
    From care and want and toil,
When dewy eve her curtain draws
    Over the day's turmoil.

"In the low chant of wakeful birds,
    In the deep weltering flood,
In whispering leaves, these solemn words—
    'God made us all for good!'

"All true, all faultless, all in tune,
    Creation's wondrous choir,
Opened in mystic unison,
    To last till time expire.

"And still it lasts: by day and night,
    With one consenting voice
All hymn Thy glory, Lord, aright,
    All worship and rejoice."

These verses of Keble's are so full of refreshment for the weary mind as well as for the fearful heart, I have copied them for you, for I think there is no refreshment for a tired mind like that which nature supplies, and surely this is one reason why our

Saviour made such frequent use of the beauty of God's world. And there is such a tender mindfulness for those of His children whose seeing of Nature's loveliness is bounded by limited out-looks, in His frequent use of types that are freighted with significance, even to those who live shut in by the brick walls of crowded cities.

For scarce one of us is too poor to own a plant; and whoever watches the unfolding of a flower can hear a voice from God. We can all feel the breath of the wind, too, and see the face of the sky. And even though it be but a patch of blue, we can study its changing hues, and there is space enough for clouds to float, space enough to catch the golden light of sunset, the rosy glory of sunrise: space enough for stars to twinkle. And these bits of nature have each a speech of their own, and if we fail to hear, we miss a part of the blessing the Lord has made a free gift to every dweller on this earth of His.

When next you are weary in mind or body, test the truth of this, and go and have a talk with Nature. Even if it be no more than a skyward look through the frame of a window casement; for though your gaze is limited, God's sky is boundless.

As for the lesson the lilies and the birds teach of our Heavenly Father's providing care, there is no need for me to guide you to it. Verily, it is an arch spanning like that sign in the sky—the bow of promise—from the land of fearfulness and doubt over to the peaceful shore of trust, and I would fain bid you note the tenderness that like a flower-strewn pathway, leads on to the after-part of the chapter which deals with the seeking of God's kingdom.

How plain it becomes that, in *that* seeking consists in part the being "rich toward God."

Think—every day we ask for these riches when we pray, "Thy kingdom come." And we can only obtain them as we give our souls to God, beseeching Him to fill them with His fulness, helping us to obey Him, and manifesting to us, that our soul's true life is a resurrection-life, hence it demands death to self and self-seeking, because we seek a kingdom that is not of this world, but "rich toward God." Rich, with no very great things, but with the little daily self-denials, the speaking a cheerful word when the heart is weary, the patient, steady performance of duties that come with every returning day—little things, I repeat, and yet they contain the riches with which God is well pleased. For if rendered in the *obedience* of faith, they lead on to the being "holy and without blame before Him in love." No wonder our hearts fail when we think of the "full consecration" such a serving of the Lord requires, for we fall so far backward, even when we are striving to reach onward.——But that is the part we are not to think of, for our only hope of final victory is the looking away from self—*Up*, all the time, to our King. And if our gaze is thus fixed on Him, we will have no time to think of ourselves, we will be every moment occupied in the doing "our duty in that state wherein it has pleased God to call us." A state of lowliness of mind as we learned from our Saviour's words, to which I said we would return, for we both felt we needed to "look deep" before we found the real heart of the lowly, the "blessed poor in spirit," to whom is promised, "theirs is the kingdom of Heaven."

The "poor in spirit"? Who are they? What does the word mean, when used in its spiritual sense?

Thus you ask—and I reply. To be poor in spirit we must know and feel our poorness, and hence our entire dependence upon God; this is the essence of Scriptural meekness, and it implies the recognition of the truth that if there be anything in us, *we* did not originate that goodness, but it is a gift from the One of all goodness. The history of Moses, the man called "the meekest among men," brings out this as clearly as sunlight brings out and sharply defines against the blue sky the network of the leafless branches that are the crown of tree-tops in winter. You remember how Moses acknowledged he was *nothing* in himself. "And Moses said unto God, Who am I, that I should go unto Pharaoh, and that I should bring forth the children of Israel out of Egypt?" "And God said unto Moses, *I am that I am.* . . . . Thus shalt thou say unto the children of Israel, I Am hath sent me unto you"—and again, "Moses said unto the Lord, O, my Lord, I am not eloquent . . . . but am slow of speech, and of a slow tongue." "And the Lord said unto him, Who hath made man's mouth? .... Have not I, the Lord? .... Now, therefore, go, and I will be with thy mouth, and teach thee what thou shalt say." No room left for pride, for self-importance—all is of God.

No lesson in the Bible seems to me so full of true lowliness of heart, or more plainly proves that the recognition of "poverty of spirit is the law of the kingdom of Heaven." God grant it may be graven on our hearts, for then it will waken a knowledge of His goodness and presence, revealing that all we have of love, thought, aspiration, and power comes from Him ; and this will so fill us with a sense of gratitude, that even here below we will know something of the happiness and the blessedness of Heaven. It will be a knowledge, too, that leads to the " Cleft in the Rock," where we may flee for shelter amid the troubles and the fears, the anxieties and the changes of this mortal existence, and spite the perils and the darkness, seeking shelter there, we may abide in "quietness and confidence," for the Lord is our Strength and our All.

Take "heart of grace," then, dear H——, and go forward, remembering it is not your weak, insufficient self that can accomplish the work of either becoming "rich toward God," or of leading *self* forth "out of Egypt," but the "I Am will be with thee." He will work *in* you that which you are to work *out*. To aid you in the accomplishment of this, I copy a thought from Mrs. Monsell which has helped me.

"Get a real living faith in the power of the transformed life in you: we hang back too much in our own nothingness instead of having a loving confidence in the power of the Holy Ghost to re-create us in Christ Jesus. This confidence is the fruit of a deeper humility, and a growing simplicity. .... All you need strive for is to love God more, more singly and simply: to still the human actings and impulses of your being in Him: to love His will for you in every little, as well as in every great thing, and to bound all your wishes and outgoings within the circle of His will. Love is of God; it is a Divine gift; do not seek to crush it; seek to keep it steadfast, and seek to help others by love, and letting their love for you draw them upward and closer to God, the Fount of all love. Oh, how blessed all the inner circles of Love are, that all rise up and find their centre in God: and then shed down upon us rays of His own Divine Love and gladness! If we dwelt more in it we should ascend more quickly to Him, even in the midst of our busiest life; and He would descend upon us with the full blessedness of His own loving Presence. Dwell in that thought, 'God is Love,' and thus you will find an anchor for your soul, sure and steadfast."

Tell me, dear H——, does not all this hold the secret wherein consists the being "rich toward God"? I think it does—and I think, too, if we strive to live humbly and earnestly in the spirit of its teaching, our hearts can sing the matin and the evensong that Faber calls "The Christian's on his march to Heaven," and which, in its interblending of Faith, Hope, and Love, is full of the soul's best riches—"the abiding three."

"Blest is the Faith, divine and strong,
   Of thanks, and praise, an endless fountain,
Whose life is one perpetual song,
   High up the Saviour's holy mountain.

" Blest is the Hope that holds to God—
    In doubt and darkness still unshaken,
  And sings along the heavenly road,
    Sweetest, when most it seems forsaken.

" Blest is the Love that cannot love
    Aught that earth gives of best and brightest;
  Whose raptures thrill like saints above,
    Most when its earthly gifts are lightest.

" Blest is the Time that in the eye
    Of God its hopeful watch is keeping,
  And grows into eternity,
    Like noiseless trees when men are sleeping."

BREAD UPON THE WATERS.

"Cast thy bread upon the waters: for thou shalt find it after many days."

Ecc. ii. 1.

"Keep on sowing,
God will cause the seed to grow
 Faster than your knowing;
Nothing e'er is sown in vain
 If, His voice obeying,
You look upward for the rain
 And falter not in praying."

V.

BREAD UPON THE WATERS

"CAST thy bread upon the waters, for thou shalt find it after many days." This is the golden text that headed a Sabbath-school paper, on a June Sunday not long ago. And as I strove—aided by the band of bright young maidens who formed my class—to find its heart of meaning, it occurred to me that our findings might prove to you, dear H——, a practical supplement to "Thoughts on Work," and so I pass them on.

The explanation of the verse as given by commentators has never satisfied me. I think it holds a much broader and fuller significance than that which merely links it to the doing of kindly deeds, and in seeking this, I did with it much as I would have done with a bunch of fragrant violets. I divided it, giving part to one, and part to another of my scholars, bidding them all find the inner meaning that clusters around Bible words as fragrance breathes out in sweet odors from flowers.

"Cast thy bread," was the share that fell to Emily Gray; "upon the waters," Fannie Buck's; "for thou shalt find it," Ellen Jordan's; Grace Flint's, "after many days."

The other members of the class were to aid in the interpretations in a general way, as a band of singers make up a chorus.

"Cast thy bread." Emily Gray lingered over the word *cast* only long enough to picture, in the glowing language that belongs to youth, a generous sower giving of his very best,—even his bread which is called "the staff of life."

As to what that bread meant she entered more into detail, for it is a very full word as used in Scripture.

"Give us our daily bread." "That is what we ask the Heavenly Father to bestow," thus Emily said, and though she was a new comer into the fold of Christ she already well knew the followers of the Lord Jesus when they use the word bread, are to think of something deeper than the mere nourishment and sustenance of the body—though surely that is one of its meanings. She knew they who hunger in the Gospel sense interpret the words as asking: "Give us the Bread of Thy strength, the gift of Thy grace." And that as the soul is more than the body, we should give the pre-eminence in our thoughts and prayers to spiritual nourishment rather than to physical strength. If this is what the Gospel bread signifies, does not the command, "cast thy bread," refer to a giving, that reaches deep as the wants of the soul, full as much as it does to the providing for the destitute? I think it does.

As Emily dwelt on this bread of heart-kindness—which is in the power of all to give—and which imbues all sweet charities with the tenderness of a sympathy that far out-runs in value mere material aid, the word bread became luminous with Heavenly radiance, for, so plain she made the truth that the leaven that leaveneth is *Love*. She bade us note, too, the significance of this spiritual bread as interlinked by association with life's discipline, using by way of illustration the ever-recurring harvest-time parable.

First, the ripened grain, reaped with sharp sickle, separated by the stroke of heavy flail—wheat from chaff, and then ground by swift wheel that the very heart of it may be made ready to supply food for thousands. Yes, her mind grasped in all its fulness this nature-taught lesson, that if we would give our very best broadcast, it must cost us something, requiring, perchance, like the grain, to be perfected for use by mower's sickle, thresher's flail, and crushing wheel! It is Robertson who writes: "Tenderness is got by suffering, both physical and mental. This was Christ's own qualification for sympathy. 'We have not an High-Priest which cannot be touched with the feeling of our infirmities: but was in all points tempted as we are.' Would you give something beyond commonplace consolation to a wounded spirit? Would you minister to doubt, to the loneliness of life?—then you must suffer—being tempted." To return to Emily Gray's explanation of the words, she maintained that they implied, that all must cast forth something, and that there was evil bread as well as good. Hence we must be either scattering pure thoughts, gentle deeds, upward-helping aspirations that are born out of Love, or evil thoughts, towering ambitions, and unlovely deeds. And then she asked—"Would the evil as well as the good, come floating back to us again, like drift-wood on the sea of time?"

Close following this last thought of Emily's, and as an echo of it, came Fannie Buck's definition of "upon the waters,"—for she summed it up in a brief but meaningful quotation from Bryant's poem:

> "A Mighty Hand, from an exhaustless urn,
> Pours forth the never-ending Flood of Years
> Among the nations. . . . .
> They gather up again and softly bear,
> All the sweet lives that late were overwhelmed,
> . . . . All that in them was good,
> Noble, and truly great, and worthy of love."

My turn to speak to these earnest-hearted girls came then. Do you wonder I pointed their thoughts to our Saviour's use of the word bread? "Jesus said, ... Verily, verily, I say unto you, ... My Father giveth you the true Bread from Heaven: For the Bread of God is He which cometh down from Heaven and giveth His life unto the world."—"And Jesus said unto them, I am the Bread of Life. .... I am that Bread of Life. .... This is the Bread which cometh down from Heaven, that a man may eat thereof, and not die. I am the living Bread."—"And He took Bread, and gave thanks, and brake it, and gave unto them, saying, This is my body which is given for you."

Bread, a type of Life!—Resurrection, Life!—For though as the two disciples walked toward Emmaus, Jesus Himself "drew near and went with them," they knew Him not, till, when "as He sat at meat with them, He took bread, and blessed and brake it, and gave to them: and their eyes were opened." .... And "the Lord was known of them in the breaking of the Bread."

While not within the confines of the text which is the index of this meditation, I cannot refrain from sharing with you the thoughts that grow out of this special revelation of the risen Christ, and which must always be associated with the "breaking of Bread." For, to quote Canon Westcott, "that which was enacted on the evening of the first Lord's day has been fulfilled, and is fulfilled, no less surely and tenderly through the experience of all believers. Christ draws near to us now, as to those unknown wayfarers, with purposes of love."

"Christ draws near to us when in the sacred intercourse of friendship we speak of our highest hopes and of our greatest sorrows .... and talk openly of that which we know to lie deepest in our nature."

"Christ draws near to us at the sad season when He seems to have been finally taken away, if we are not ashamed to confess, in the apparent disappointment of our hopes, that we are still His disciples."

"Christ draws near to us when at some solemn appeal, we pause on our journey, and stand in wondering sorrow perhaps, not knowing what answer to give to an unexpected and importunate questioner whose words touch us to the quick."

"Christ draws near to us at the very crisis when we strive to give distinctness to our misgivings and to our difficulties. He asks us to speak freely to Him, and accepts the most imperfect confession of a sincere faith as the basis of His tender discipline."

"Christ draws near to us when humbly

and honestly we ponder His word. The study is difficult—far more difficult than we commonly suppose, and far more fruitful—but He illuminates the dark places, and through a better understanding of the letter guides us to a warmer sympathy with the spirit."

"Christ draws near to us when we take gladly the reproof which reveals to us our ignorance and our coldness, and resolutely strive to retain in our company the Teacher, who by sharp methods has made us better able to see the truth."

"Christ draws near to us when we are bidden to draw near to Him at His Holy Table, and there gives us back with His blessing the offerings which we have brought to Him."

"So Christ draws near to us, or at least He waits to draw near to us, in the manifold changes of our mortal life, near to us as we go in and go out in the fulfilment of our common duties, near to us when we are reassembled in our homes, near to us in the time of trial, and in the hour of death."

This is a wide digression—but you will not think it too wide, if it helps to bring

Him—the Lord of Life—nearer and yet nearer. We left our pondering on the casting of "bread on the waters" just as we had come to the knowledge that our every deed and thought is in very truth either a flower or a weed cast on that broad flowing current—the years of our lives.

Flowers and weeds! All to float back again either in blessed peace-giving remembrances, or in bitter remorse, wakening regrets as the tide turns, and the out-going changes into the in-coming. For while in one sense if we are Christians, we are not to look back—but only forward—yet in another, as long as we stay here on earth, it holds true—"as ye sow, so shall ye reap."

And now, I will not tarry over the other "meanings" my girls found, for they are so plain-sighted you know them already. I only note the foregone by way of help toward the "sowing" that is a part of the blessed ministry that belongs to the daily home and social life that surrounds you— and the still greater work you have to do in the heart, where is planted the root that up-springs into outward life—remember, it is the root at which God looks. His eye sees beyond the outward, and it is what we *are*, that He regards, not what we *seem* to be.

And, in this heart-garden there need be no weed sowing, if we plant according to His bidding in "faith and patience," remembering love to Christ is the sure root of love to our neighbor, just as it is the foundation of service, and the rule of service is thoughtfulness. Hence if we are really to work for Christ "we must consider more patiently than we commonly do the requirements of those whom we have to serve. For there is no one method for all. Here, there is need for the tenderest simplicity: there, of the wisest authority: there, of the ripest result of long reflection."

This extract will, I think, give you in suggestion what you ask for when you say: "Please add a page all hedged in by thoughts of woman's work for woman," for it bounds *all* service by "love, considerate thoughtfulness, and self-surrender."

As for woman's special work, we who live in this nineteenth century are so richly blessed in the recognition of our work, and thoughts of and for it are so multiplied, I have not so much as one fresh blossom to offer, by way of suggestion on the subject. Nevertheless, I will bid you remember, for those who have "no definite work" there is always "the indefinite" calling out to be done. And if your lot in life is cast among those who need make no effort for personal support, it in no way shuts you out from service, for God has given every soul a work to do for Him, even if it be no more than the following up the "opportunities" others are forced to pass by, because, having a set task to perform, limits out-reaching effort, and yet it is a fact that those whose lives are most full of the "must be done" are the very ones who are wont to be ready for still more service.

What do I mean by following up opportunities?—The ample means for mental culture, and the sunshine that has enfolded your life, suggests a reply. For if you gather up the fragments of knowledge—and of brightness by which you have been blessed, and go forth among those less favored, and share these fragments with them, you will know my meaning. Only be very sure to let them be true bits of sunshine. There are so many rays of light waiting to be thus sent forth on errands of comfort, and often their delivery demands no more than the giving of a flower, or the meeting some lonely heart with a kindly smile, or a tender word of cheer and good-will.

And these "messages" involve no elaborate system of organization, but are best offered simply and quietly. But simple though they be, they do demand the life-warming conviction that can only come when they are "done unto Him." If thus done—wonderful as it seems—it may be His will to take your deeds as He did the multiplying loaves, and bless them into portions for many!

In the matter of more practical service among women—your sisters—there always will be work and work to be done by those who have ample means; for as long as this world lasts, it is written, "The poor shall never cease out of the land, therefore I command thee, saying, Thou shalt open thine hand wide to thy poor and thy needy" (Deut. xv. 11).

Yes—"the poor ye have with you always,"

thus our Saviour said, too, and I think He meant us to remember when we pray for "daily bread," that "giving and receiving" are so interwoven in His blessed dispensation that as we ask bread *from* Him, we are to offer bread *to* Him by living in daily fulfilment of the spirit of His command, "Inasmuch as ye do it unto the least of these my brethren, *ye do it unto Me.*"

You ask me to mention some of the simple ways which I have found most successful in approaching hearts. Among them, flowers fill a large place—their language is so universal; and the lending of books, too, I have found very helpful—notice I say *lending*, for that gives a sense of sharing our good things with others that making a gift sometimes fails in. And in the matter of books you will be surprised by the quick response you will meet to thoughts of beauty—and higher things. I have a copy of "The Story of Ida," well-nigh worn out by its much going to and fro among those whom we are wont to call the "poorer classes," though often I think they are the richer! You will find too, if you try it, an hour or so spent several times a week in helping young girls, whose lot in life is to be "working women"—to find a motive in even the most homely tasks, will prove a very fruitful opening, that points on to spiritual things. And never yet have I met one so dull but that after a little upward leading, they have caught a ray of light from old Herbert's words:

> "Teach me, my God and King,
>   In all things Thee to see,
> And what I do in anything,
>   To do it as for Thee.
>
> "All may of Thee partake:
>   Nothing can be so mean
> Which with this tincture—for Thy sake—
>   Will not grow bright and clean.
>
> "A servant with this clause,
>   Makes drudgery divine:
> Who sweeps a room as for Thy laws
>   Makes that and th' action fine.
>
> "This is the famous stone
>   That turneth all to gold:
> For that which God doth touch and own
>   Cannot for less be told."

And now passing on to a class a grade higher in social rank—think of the many young women who are striving to support themselves, and to whom a few lessons from either yourself or a good master—which your means would enable you to supply—would be a life-long boon. Then, too, one can, even by a hint or two, so help those who have not had the advantages we have had in acquiring skill with their hands to execute the dainty bits of work by which women can help themselves nowadays.

An hour's talk on color, will serve to guide a quick-minded girl from a crude use of mis-matching tints to a soft blending of harmonious shades that will increase the value of her work to double its aforetime compensation.

But your own heart will tell you better than I can, how to help others who are struggling after the material support which encompasses you as bountifully as the air you breathe.

If now and then, in the seeking thus to cast your "bread upon the waters," you fail, do not miss the lesson of failure, for it is a lesson well worth learning, if it leads to more dependence on God. Yes—the very fact of failure shows us " that we have expected too much from ourselves, and too little from God."

"We have set ourselves to do this or that *for Him*, instead of trusting Him to do it *for us*, and then we have said, 'Alas, I have no power,' forgetting that He *has*, whereas our plea should be, 'Now, Lord, the work is Thine; how can I dare to doubt the power is Thine also, even to sanctify me wholly and preserve me blameless unto the coming of Thy Son.'"

I remember once reading these words, and as they have stayed in my heart helpfully, I think they may also aid you, so I pass them on, for it is one way of "casting bread on the waters," this sending truths that have helped us, on to others. Hence I will add to it Mrs. Browning's heart and purpose-questioning lines:

"What are we set on earth for?—say, to toil—
  Nor seek to leave thy tending of the vines,
  For all the heat thro' day, till it declines,
  And Death's wild curfew shall from work assoil.
  God did anoint them with His odorous oil,
  To wrestle, not to reign: and He assigns
  All thy tears over, like pure crystallines,
  For younger fellow-workers of the soil,

To wear for amulets. So others shall
Take patience, labor, to their heart and hand,
From thy heart and thy hand, and thy brave cheer,
And God's grace fructify, through thee to all.
The least flower with a brimming cup may stand
And share its dew-drops with another near."

CHASTENING.

"Whom the Lord loveth He chasteneth. . . . . If ye endure chastening God dealeth with you as with sons."

HEB. xii. 6, 7.

"Whatsoe'er betideth, night or day,
  Know His love for thee provideth good alway."

Remember,

"Just as sweetness comes from the bark of the cinnamon when bruised, so can the spirit of the Cross of Christ bring beauty and holiness and peace out of the bruised and broken heart."

ROBERTSON.

VI.

CHASTENING.

YOU ask me, dear H——, to tell you in detail, what I meant, when, as we pondered on "quietness," I referred to God's love in chastening.

You say, the verse, "Whom the Lord loveth He chasteneth," is dull and cold to you, all void of meaning.

Ah! how can I make it warm and life-like. How can I open your eyes to see, it is Love that leads to His infinite rest, even though it be by a path, tear-strewn all the way. And yet, unless you do come to know this, you miss a blessed part of your heritage as a child of God. For, no one can doubt that the Christian is chastened, and that he has a cross to carry; the Bible is full of the lesson. At the same time it makes plain the truth, that the preparation God makes for all, saints and sinners alike, is equal. But—and here comes in the difference, that up-wells in refreshment from the "brook in the way"—while it is true that God loves all, His love only reaches a few because it is appropriated by but few. Hence, while He sends what may be chastening to all, it becomes such only to those who are in the right spirit, for they only have the heart of faith that *knows* love is there, even though hidden from sight.

Do you catch my meaning? All are His sheep, but some do not, because they will not, hear His Voice. So that practically He only leads His own; and in regard to the leading of chastening, I do not believe when we enter upon the Christian life we enter under a new dispensation, but rather into a new relation. We change toward God. He does not change toward us. He deals with us just as He dealt before, but where, as formerly, our hearts were like smooth-surfaced stones, from which the rain ran off in wasted streamlets, now they have become rich earth, and it falls on soil ready to absorb its every drop, and we find what before was a trial crushing us, has become a chastening rod, for we *endure* chastening. This is the secret of God's dealing with us as with sons. For remember, it is our position toward God that brings us into a child's place. And acquiescence in His will is the child's own special mark of sonship, the proof of our being in harmony with His dealing. So you see it is not that any new trials and struggles have come; but, some are met for the first time, we conquer some that before conquered us—we *take up* our cross: we bear it for the first time, but it is the same old cross that crushed us before we came to Christ. To quote from one who thought much on this subject: "The call that bade us come to Him, was not a call into a new phenomenal and objective life, but into harmony with our present life. It is a practical call which brings us into no new trials and duties, but it brings us into harmony with the old."

In other words,

"The cross on Golgotha will never save thy soul,
The cross in thine own heart alone can make it whole."

I think, too, we mistake when we speak of God's loving particularly, in our hours of trouble, for God's love is unchanging.

It is written, "I am He that changes not." But troubles open our eyes to see His love more clearly, that there is no doubt of, and love means more too, when we are in trouble.

But I will not tarry over these thoughts; the simple statement is enough, that I believe the "new life spoken of in the Bible is a new spirit in the old life." A sinner has trials, fights with doubts, is disquieted, longs for Heaven, has everything of trouble that a Christian has, and more too—for to a Christian there is a peace in trial, a strength given with which to meet it. The fight comes to each, but the Christian only has the armor.

As to the denying of self, which is included in your thought of chastening. Yes, surely we should deny ourselves, give up everything that keeps Christ out of the first place in our hearts and love, but this is merely because "we are like patients now, on the sick-list as it were, and must wait until we reach Heaven and perfect spiritual health before it will do for us to indulge ourselves."

Does all this seem to you a bit like preaching, a bit like bidding you stand in the vestibule, when, what you want is to come close to the altar—what you want is to feel the firm grasp of a faith that shines with illumining light through the darkness of grief, whispering, though the natural heart cries out against it, "God's will *is* best."

You can only find this light as you bow before His will, then the sense of nearness will come too, for when the heart has thus bowed, it *knows the* love of *chastening*, knows that fellowship with Christ which is sorrow's crown of consecration—and which is all beyond the power of words to tell.

You will remember the cross we are called to bear, if we would be His disciples, is a *daily* cross—and this seems to prove that it is *self*, the self we are to overcome by daily inward struggle with the evil in our hearts. Thus when we speak of chastening, we mean not only outward trials that all lookers-on recognize as trials, but the inward subduing, the fight of faith in the soul. Without the recognition of this inner discipline, we lose the essence of what chastening really means, for we narrow it to the compass of the visible trials, the tangible troubles which are often but hints of the heart-chastening, the self-conquering, through which we learn to yield our wills to God's.

In all this, how tenderly the Christ is our great Exemplar, for "the way in which He walked to His glorification is the way we must walk to our regeneration." And, if it be sometimes a "Calvary way," we know He trod every step before us; we may hear at every moment His Voice, saying, "Follow thou Me!" Do you believe this? If you do, then I will give you a little hymn to sing—

"The clouds hang heavy around my way, I cannot see:
But through the darkness, I believe God leadeth me.
'Tis sweet to keep my hand in His, while all is dim:
To close my weary, aching eyes, and follow Him.
Through many a thorny path He leads my tired feet,
Through many a path of tears to go, but it is sweet
To know that He is close to me—my God, my guide—
He leadeth me, and so I walk, quite satisfied."

In a former meditation we dwelt on our Lord as "A Man of Sorrows"; but the reference I now make to "His acquaintance with grief," is simply, that by recalling His sufferings we may be better able to see the good of, and the need for sorrow. For, the believing that there is a need, even though here on earth we may never clearly see its "why," is the only way by which we can meet the universal existence of sorrow and pain, as, spite the anguish they cost, still blessings, because they are encompassed with God's love. And, even then, with all our believing, how hard it is to be reconciled !

I suppose one reason why we cannot understand it now, is, that if God made the why of His dealings all plain, faith's work in the soul would be so lessened ; then there is the fact, that we are too much in the sorrow now. But, when the cloud is at last lifted, then we will see, and understand with never a shadow falling across the unbroken blue. Yet though we wait for this *full* knowledge, broad glints of light even now fall across the "mystery of sorrow." And by the radiance of this kindling of our darkness, how many a helpful lesson we learn. And since the great object of life here is to fit us for life *There*, we may rest assured that God will do this fitting in the best way, even if it be by laying the axe to the root of our heart's dearest earthly treasures, for the promise is, "Blessed is the man

Thou chasteneth and teacheth out of Thy law, O Lord."

We must not overlook in our thoughts on chastening the great mercy of the fact, that we do not know the way, or when our trials will come; for if we did, how we would strive to anticipate and prevent them, how we would often delay God's work of grace in the soul. This hiding of the *why* of His Providence, and sometimes the hiding too of His Presence, is, I think, one of the lessons God teaches us through the history of His servant Moses—for Moses' experience is so full, a very "burning bush" of suggestions, helping us when we seem all shut in by sorrows. "He said, Thou canst not see my face and live."—"I will cover thee with my Hand while I pass by." Let the comfort of this enfold your heart, when great sorrow comes again, for it bids you rest assured, even if you cannot see God's face, you can know "He will cover you with His Hand." His own Word tells you this.—And then the afterward! When His glory has passed by, then you shall see the behind part—then—when His Providence has done its work in your soul, you will know something of the love of the *why*, which passes far beyond any aforetime knowledge you ever have had yet. And, in the blessed Hereafter you will know all the reason of the why. Ah! it is worth the waiting for!—Think when the night of our trial time is passed what a sunrising it will be! And for now—if you have sought shelter in the "Rock cleft," then, the very glory of His passing by, will be enough for you to trim your lamp by. So sit no longer in the dark, but turn the leaves of the Book, and read the gracious words traced therein for just such chastened ones as you and me.

Tell me, do you not find them broad and full enough to span your every need? Do not the chastenings which at first seemed so grievous, become sweet tokens of your Heavenly Father's care?

I am sure they do, if you accept God's will as your will, however His chastening comes.

For His way of training hearts is very different with His different children. Some are called to part with their dearest, whose going puts out the sunshine in their hearts and homes; while others are disciplined by the strengthening of their dear earthly ties;

for by prosperity as well as by affliction the Lord chastens His children, and for both trials, the trial of love and the trial of possession, there is the same balm, the balm that lies in prayer, for those who know God listens, and that,

> " The Saviour giveth
> Daily strength . . . .
> . . . . Ask not then, ' When or How,'
> Only bow."

And now, by way of closing of this many-paged meditation on chastening and its lessons, I copy for you a Scotch hymn that often comes to my memory when I sit alone in the gloaming, and it never comes without, like a hand-clasp of good cheer, bidding me go on my way amid the shadows of earth's changes with a heart calm to meet them because they are ordered by God's will. I wonder will it hold the same comfort for you?

> " There are blossoms that hae budded, been blicked o' the cauld,
> And lammies that hae perished, because they left the fauld;

But cower ye in aneath His wings who deed upon the tree,
And gathers in His bosom helpless weans like you and me.
In the warl there's tribulation, in the warl there is woe.
Then brighten up your armor, and be happy as ye gang,
Though your sky be often clouded, it winna be for lang."

8

THE AGE WE LIVE IN.

"We all with open face, beholding as in a glass the glory of the Lord, are changed into the same image from glory to glory, even as by the Spirit of the Lord."
2 COR. iii. 18.

"Says God : Who comes to me an inch through doubtings dim,
In blazing light I do approach a yard toward Him."
ORIENTAL POETRY.

VII.

THE AGE WE LIVE IN.

I AM in full sympathy with you, dear H——, in regard to what you say about "religious truth and controversy."

Yes, you are right, the very air nowadays seems pulsating with what is called "new theology," "progressive thought," "advanced views," and "widening out-looks."

But while I agree with you that there are grave dangers in all this, I think there are great blessings, too, and always there is the safety-place to which we may flee, for *"God's Truth is one and abiding."*

Nevertheless, the present bewilderment in the breaking up of "creed authority" must present a serious phenomenon to all earnest minds, marked as it is by modern individualism.

"How are we to account for it?" you ask.

The universally acknowledged fact that

"religion is an indispensable part of man's moral and mental out-fit," suggests one reply : and two causes have contributed to deepen this conviction in modern times. Canon Liddon tells us : "The first is the subjective spirit of the age which insists on looking at truth, not as it is, in its utter independence of the mind of man, but as it presents itself to man's mind, or rather as man's mind in very varying moods approaches it. This spirit, while it has weakened the public hold upon creeds and Scriptures, has directed attention with an intensity unknown before our day, to the needs of the human mind, and among them to its supreme need of a religion."

He further writes : "The indispensableness of religion to human life has also been forced on the mind of this generation by a deeper study of history." You will see the truth of this statement, if you sum up the most important historical events, for you will then see how "the most profound and far-reaching changes have really turned upon religious questions."

Recall, too, that saying of Goethe's, "The deepest subject in the history of the world and of mankind, and that to which all others are subordinate, is the conflict between faith and unbelief."

Realizing all this, we see interest in religion is inevitable among the thoughtful of our day and generation. But the practical question is, "What is it that man seeks in seeking religion?" And this brings us to one of the "signs of the time" that troubles you, because it seems lacking in the earnest reverence with which you fain would have all sacred topics encompassed.

You say, "The most holy truths, from familiar discussion have come to be tossed about in conversation with a careless irreverence that thinks more of the theories and opinions to be maintained than of the vital truth that makes their real value."

Yes—I know this is so, but, for you, as well as for myself, it need not trouble us if we keep within the Shadow of His Hand, within the sound of His "still, small voice," whose faintest whisper can calm all the din and turmoil of mere opinion.——And what are opinions but a result of views, and hence limited by spiritual outlook. It is well to remember this, for in the matter of "religious views"—which I think a strictly accurate philosophical expression—new impressions and ideas come crowding in on us, just as they do when we look out over some wide land or sea view, and need to wait, before we can adjust "near and far" into their own true places—for so we need to wait, before we pronounce decidedly on subjects of which even the wisest are slow in judging.

And as we wait, let us remember, "there may be absolute and higher truth of which what we know is only the shadowed outline; we cannot reach it now—but it is there, ready for us behind the veil."

And at best, what can we prove? Tennyson's words are so true:

" For nothing worthy proving can be proven,
Nor yet disproven: wherefore then be wise,
And cling to Faith, beyond the forms of Faith!
She reels not in the storm of warring words,
She brightens at the clash of 'Yes' and 'No.'
She sees the Best that glimmers thro' the Worst,
She feels the Sun is hid but for a night,
She spies the Summer thro' the winter bud,
She tastes the fruit before the blossom falls,
She hears the lark within the songless egg,
She finds the fountain, where they wailed, 'Mirage!'"

Hence, I bid you hold your mind open to truth, even though it may come to you at the cost of your pulling down a hoard of maxims, and close clinging to the *letter* of the law rather than the *spirit*—a state of mind that I call, for lack of a better term, a sort of framing in of your traditional conscience. Do not infer from this that I mean *speculation* is truth, or that systems of thought are to be received as God's revelation. But what I want to recognize is, that there is danger in a too determined clinging to the "old ways," as well as danger in an undue reaching out after the new. For the one is apt, as we grow in years, to develop into superstition, while the other, without prayerful watching, will end in scepticism.

Let us then, dear H——, hold fast to the "faith once delivered," but let us "add to faith, knowledge." And a generous willingness to welcome what of good has grown out of the wide study and enlarged thought of the present age. As I write this, I feel I need the warning, perchance, more than you do, for I am a very conservative by nature, prone to abjure theories, and I will confess it has always, and does now seem to me, that those who simply and trustfully do the *present* duty, are wont to be clearer-sighted in the spiritual life, than those whose vision ranges far. For, there is always the risk, that in searching for great things, we may overlook the present, and the command is for day by day living. Nevertheless, the world has need for the far seekers, as well as the near, and to whichever party we belong, it is well for us to be wide awake to the good contained in the other.

But let us turn from these ponderings, which savor of unrest in a certain way, and instead of them, listen for a while to the whispers of the voice in the soul—and, if those whispers lead us round to the same thoughts, we need not fear to follow their guidance, for it is the Holy Spirit that leads by them.

How still they are, these Spirit whispers, and so powerful! Silent as sunlight, yet transmuting the material into the spiritual, bidding us penetrate like the warm rays of sunshine beyond and beneath the visible. That is a real "modern day" thought, do you tell me? Well, if it is, think of the beneath, where there is so much concealed! Think how diamonds lie hidden from sight year after year, and gold, deep imbedded under fathoms of rock and loam. Think, too, of the springs of living waters that are locked for centuries silent in fastnesses of the hills, and the deep caverns of the earth—and all these treasures are waiting for some touch, like that of Moses' rod, to set them free.

These thoughts are types, and yet types even when Bible-culled are well-nigh empty, till they become meaningful because of some linking with real life, that serves to illuminate their spiritual as well as their material side.

And, the "still, small Voice," how often it guides memory back over a silent stretch of years to some such life-like remembrance.

This very minute it brings to my mind a simple "all true" story, that holds in suggestion a lesson full of the portrayal of God's overruling Love revealed by the bringing to light one of the "beneath things." And because it points beyond the visible, I pass it on to you.

It leads to a far distant land and a time,

by-gone by many years. Our surroundings are all strange, "cannons to right, and cannons to left" of us. The siege of Sebastopol is at its height. The brave, undaunted band of battle-marred soldiers who for long have guarded one special point grow less in number with every passing hour. Long fasting—and the deadlier foe, thirst—doing a more fatal work than cannon-ball and bursting shell. And yet, in the hearts of those brave men hope died hard—but, thirst is cruel, and with it came despair—when—— Hark!—through the parting air once again Russian shell follows shell, once again the earth is rent and torn, the crimson tide of life-blood flows fast—when—lo!—from the clefted sod up-wells a bubbling fountain!—water—pure and cool! And that life-spring, set free by an enemy's missile of death, never once failed while the siege lasted. To scores and scores of thirst-parched men it proved an almoner of life and refreshment. There is no need for me to point the meaning of this story, it tells its own lesson, and yet such stories are well to recall when one has been dwelling on the environment of the present day. For they tell us, escape from the trammel of "why and wherefore" is found in a firm trust in the overruling care of Him who can cause water to up-spring in the desert, who can say to the wildest storm of doubt, "Be still," and there will be "a great calm."

And now, here we are round again to the fact that speculation, the spirit of questioning, like a huge interrogation-point on a blank page is the atmosphere of the age we live in. We cannot put this truth by—and would we if we could? I think not, for, thank God, if the waves that toss this questioning age be turbulent and restless, as mid-ocean billows, yet hearts and minds have grown broader by the very tossing. Faith's boundaries have widened, spite the fact that sometimes they *seem* narrowing. We have come to know,

> " The love of God is broader
>   Than the measure of man's mind,
> And the heart of the Eternal
>   Is most wonderfully kind."

We have come to a clearer insight of the lines of progress, and see through perspective the real advance that has followed the learning that where the questioning is *honest*, it may yield a richer harvest than that which ripens from a persistent clinging to "what one has been taught." Robert Browning expresses this in words that may seem to you somewhat harsh—still, I think you will acknowledge they are alive with the vigor of a healthy progressive life :

> " And so I live, you see,
>   Go through the world, try, prove, reject,
>   Prefer, still struggling to effect
>   My warfare : happy that I can
>   Be crossed and thwarted as a man,
>   Not left in God's contempt apart
>   With ghastly smooth life, dead at heart,
>   Tame in earth's paddock as her prize.
>   . . . . . .
>   Thank God, no paradise stands barred
>   To entry, and I find it hard
>   To be a Christian, as I said."

If all this involves a time of spiritual up-stirring, surely we can rest satisfied that a *higher order* will blossom out of it, just as the earth that is most stirred by plow and furrow, in the end brings forth the fullest fruitage.

As to the matter of unsettled creeds, if

we remember creeds, even the very best of them, are of man's making, how many a note of discord would be quieted, because louder than them all, sounds the Voice of Him, who summed up in so brief a space the first and great foundation principle of Christian life—love—love to God, and love to man.

Love!—it touches the key-note of a creed I pray God you and I may in very truth be able to preface with an "I believe."

Love!—ah, if that one word in all its fulness could stand as the capital letter of all creeds, how the spirit of opposition would die out for want of nourishment, the bitterness of discussion grow warm and fragrant with the incense that haloes Christ's "Love" command; for when love is the root, little does it matter whether the flower of worship be a blossom of liturgy, or of untrammeled speech.

And—what do disputes and differences of opinion, lengthy discussions, and clashing arguments as to that most vexed and mooted question, the Hereafter, amount to, before the greater question, Is thy heart right before God?

If we can answer that, standing in the full illumining of His promise, "Unto the upright there ariseth light," we need feel no fear of this questioning, restless age, for then our anchor is *Faith*. We can calm ourselves in the thought of the strong, steady Hand at the wheel, and holding that Hand, oh, how surely we know the waves wrecking about us never for one moment mean the parting of the strong planks of the Life-Boat in which we sail. For above the clash and the roar of howling winds and breaking waves, loud and clear as the song of a lark, rings out the Lighthouse bell—"Port is near." "The Haven is sure." "Hold fast, all is well."

Yes, very well; for even now,

"The lights are gleaming from the distant shore,
  Where no billows threaten, where no tempests roar."

Does the glimmer of these lights make you long to go?

Yes—I know——many a time it is hard not to pray,

"Lord, loose the cable, let me go—"
But
"Hark the solemn answer,
 Hark the promise sure,

Blessed are the servants who to the end endure!
Yet a little longer, hope and tarry on,
Yet a little longer, weak and weary one—
More to perfect patience, to grow in faith and love,
More my strength and wisdom, and faithfulness to prove,
Then the sailing orders the captain shall bestow—
Loose the cable, let thee go."

I do not feel satisfied, dear H——, to leave this meditation without turning again for a moment to the thought that environment counts for much, hence we must meet the questions of this age we live in, for they are stirring around us like snowflakes falling thick and fast on a December storm day. Then, too, I so want you to feel the strength, the quietness, and confidence there is in meeting them with a firm trust in the great "I Am." Out of this trust comes a power that enables the mind to discriminate between doubt and speculation, as the eager search of an earnest soul after light, and doubt and speculation as a mere indulgence of spiritual self-conceit, for there is a vast difference in the two.

I recall a lesson of wisdom on this very point, and the importance of being just in the reception of what may be to us new thoughts. It was taught a company of ladies by one of God's dear saints, who went from earth to Heaven not many months ago.

Dispute ran high; the verdict pronounced on the young minister under discussion, and who had recently been called to fill a century and century-old gospel pulpit, was "too progressive," "too advanced."

Silently my old friend had listened, while one of those shrewd, yet kindly smiles that seem to belong to a fast passing generation, lit up her countenance. When at last she spoke, it was very quietly, and at first I thought her words far away from the subject.

"In my young days," thus she began, "voyagers across the wide Atlantic took passage in some staunch, white-winged sailing craft, and slow was the progress, requiring many a tack to eastward and to westward to catch every breath of the favoring wind." Just here she paused before adding: "But nowadays things are changed. Swift as a bird goes through the air, the steam-fed vessel spans the ocean miles. A voyage that once took weeks to accomplish, now fills a time brief as from one Sabbath to the next."

Then came a pause again, while the smile on her face became more tender, as after a minute she continued : " And, somehow—I am thinking, though the old ways *are good* (she was too loyal to admit a past tense), the old ways are dear, yet if I were to start tomorrow for a land beyond the sea, you would not bid me set sail in some old-time 'ship of the line.' No, you would send me forth with a 'God-speed' in the very swiftest and the surest of the modern-built vessels that ply from shore to shore.—And—I am thinking"—unconsciously she seemed to repeat the words—" we should be as open-minded in acknowledging the good progress made in the spiritual world, where religious thought is leader, as we are to acknowledge the progress made in the material." And there was not one of all that company who said " nay " to my old friend's words.

And now by way of farewell to this subject, dear H———. I will let Canon Liddon speak to you again, for I much like the way by which he tells: "If man's religious wants are to be answered, his creed must speak, not merely to his intelligence, but to his heart and will. He cannot really rest upon the most unimpeachable abstractions. He needs something warmer than the truest philosophy. He yearns to come in contact with a heart: and no religion, therefore, can really satisfy him which does not at least lead him to know and love a person. An unseen Friend, who will purify, and teach, and check, and lead, and sustain him:—that is his great necessity. And this want, this last but deepest want of man's religious life, Christianity has satisfied. As humanity, 'sitting in darkness and in the shadow of death,' pleads with the Power whom it feels, but cannot see—'Show Thou me the way that I should walk in, for I lift up my soul unto Thee.' Lo! the heavens drop down from above, and the skies pour forth righteousness. And One fairer than the children of men presents Himself to all the centuries and centuries of the world with the gracious bidding: 'Come unto Me, all ye that labor and are heavy laden, and I will give you rest'——only come."

WILDERNESS DAYS.

"Then was Jesus led up of the Spirit into the wilderness to be tempted of the devil."

MATT. iv. 1.

"O Soul of Jesus . . . .
Thy Spirit weighs the sins of man . . . .
And Thou hast struggled with it, Lord! . . . .
By the pains of Thy pure love
Grant me the gift of holy fear . . . .
Even when tempted, make me see."

FABER.

VIII.

WILDERNESS DAYS.

"I WILL bring you into the wilderness."

How like a special invitation that sounds, a special assurance of our Lord's own leading: "*I* will bring you"—but, ah! dear H——, think where it leads.

And—whether we will go or not is not asked—no, the words are, "will bring." Temptation—for that is what this wilderness typifies for us—is something we must all meet; the only thing about it that is under our control is the yielding or resisting, and that involves conflict, for it is a struggle between the evil and the good which are implanted in every heart for the development of character. And, that we may have courage for this conflict, the companionship of our Saviour in times of trial is repeatedly promised. We are even told:

"He was in all points tempted like as we are." But, ah! the difference!—He was "*without sin*"—while as for us!—who can number their sins?—Not either you or I. To return to the comfort and strength of Christ's knowing all about temptation—except the yielding to it—have you ever followed this thought of the two-foldness that runs through Christian life?—making it a condition of being "alone, yet not alone."

It shines with so bright a light on the complex truth that the Divine Helper is working with us, and yet, while our choosing good is the work of God, it is at the same time a work only accomplished through our own free determinate willingness to choose the good. This working of God and man together, stands out so clearly defined in the history of wilderness days, for truly temptations seem one of the plainest ways of revealing it, one of the most comforting too; for since our Lord was led into the wilderness, and trod every step of the way before us, if we seek His strength, the "strength made perfect in weakness," after the trial-time we, you and I, may "come up from the wilderness leaning on our Beloved." Listen to His invitation:

> " Lean on me! unchanging love
>   Shall shield thee, in my warm embrace.
> Lift up thy thoughts, thy hope's above,
>   No frowns are on thy Saviour's face.
> Art thou distressed with inward guilt
>   When secret sins rise up to view?
> Forget not then, whose blood was spilt
>   To cleanse, to sanctify, renew."
>
>   .   .   .   .   .
>
> Lean hard, my child, dismiss thy fear,
>   I will uphold."

Can you sing from your heart the last verses of this simple hymn—

> " Jesus, my Lord! I know Thy Voice,
>   On Thee with confidence I lean,
> In Life, in death, my only choice,
>   All hope, all wealth, in Thee are seen.
>
> " Here will I lean, nor doubt Thy love,
>   Or power to hold me safely up—
> With heart and hope still fixed above,
>   Humbly I'll drink Thy mingled cup."

Ah! if you can truly sing them, then, verily, the words, "come up, leaning on our Beloved," belong to you. "Come up"! the very words proclaim advance—something is gained by the wilderness sojourn. The issue of temptation is upward toward victory. For Christ has made it possible for us to meet temptation with the hope of conquering. "We Christians can dare to face it, for He has brought us both a pardon and an antidote. His cross and passion are a revelation as well as a cure. .... When dying He showed us what sin is. .... Standing beneath the Cross, we can never deem moral evil less or other than the greatest, if it be not rather the only evil. Kneeling before the Crucified, be our sense of guilt what it may, we can never despair, since the complete revelation of the malignity of sin is also and simultaneously a revelation of the Love that knows no bounds."

"It is these concrete truths, and no abstract considerations, which really keep alive in the Christian's heart an abhorrence and dread of moral evil. With that evil, even when all has been pardoned, every Christian life is, from first to last, in varying degrees a struggle. There are great conflicts, and there are periods of comparative repose; there are days of failure, as well as days of victory; there are quickenings of buoyant thankful hope, and there are hours of discouragement which is only not despair. But two things a genuine Christian never does: he never makes light of any known sin, and he never admits it to be invincible. While he constantly endeavors, by the sanctification of his desires, by entwining his affections more and more around the Source of goodness, to destroy sin in the bud, or rather in its root and principle, he is never off his guard; never surprised at new proof of his natural weakness; never disposed to underrate either his dangers or his strength. He knows that now, as eighteen centuries ago, he wrestles not against flesh and blood, but against principalities and powers that bear him no good-will: he knows that as at the first, so now, 'if any man sin we have an advocate with the Father, Jesus Christ the Righteous, and He is the propitiation for our sins.' And thus, in his inmost life, he is at once anxious and hopeful: confident, yet without presumption; alive to all that is at stake day by day, hour by hour: yet stayed upon the thought, nay, upon the felt presence of a Love which has not really left him to himself. And at last, when it seems best to that Eternal Love, the day of struggle draws to its close, and the towers of the Everlasting City come into view : the city within whose precincts intellectual error cannot penetrate, and moral failure is unknown."—"Thanks be to God who giveth us the victory through our Lord Jesus Christ."

A long extract, dear H——, which I cull from the volume, quoted often before—Canon Liddon's "Elements of Religion"—but if you read it carefully, I think you will find it none too long, for it will prove a helpful entrance to thoughts on the peculiar temptations that belong to our wilderness days. But, before we ponder them, let us pause to note the lesson of Israel's wilderness mercies and wilderness wanderings, with an application to ourselves, for since the Old Testament as well as the New is for instruction, they must hold lessons for us.

And the wilderness through which God's chosen people were brought, that they might "go up to the good land and take possession of it," surely is a very striking emblem of our spiritual experience, for remember we are the Lord's spiritual Israel, and the wilderness stands as a type of the world through which we must journey, not escaping its temptations, but overcoming them, if we are to enter "the good land of promise," the Canaan which we can only reach as we pass over Jordan!

Passing over Jordan! The meaning held in that passing, how deep it goes, reaching down to the very root of self-love and self-will. For, though the metaphors are different, the underlying truth—death to self—is the same as that to which St. Paul referred when he said, "I die daily."

The death of self-will—no wonder we come to it by the way of the wilderness, for it dies hard.

No wonder the waters of the typical Jordan are cold and dark: no wonder we dread the entering into life through death, and yet we must do it if we are to be "made conformable to His death." But it is not death of which we are to think—no, it is life—for that is what our Lord imparts to us when we have passed over Jordan. Yes, life—for the promise is, not only that we shall abide "in Him," but that He "abides in us."

Remember, out of this abiding, comes the soul's communing with God, which reveals the secret of Divine wisdom. Think—"out of the abiding of the Son with the Father flows the wealth of the Word's high knowledge. He knows—because He abides in the bosom of the Father. This is the law of intellectual life in its highest conceivable expression, in the Word, who is the Thought and Reason of God Himself: this law, then, regulates the exercise of reason from end to end of its domains: in this lies the secret of its force, the condition of its success: and we, on our lower level, we, whose reason works in the image of the Word, in whose light alone we see light, can win our intellectual way only through conformity to the primal conditions under which the Word of God moves forward to His victorious apprehensions. We can only understand that in which we abide, with which we have intimate union, to which we are ourselves conformed. . . . . The closer our contact, the surer grows our knowledge: and only out of the growing pressure of familiar intercourse can our reason gain ever-quickening activity, ever-increasing assurance. . . . . Its instinctive sympathies, its sense of security, its touches of persuasiveness, its effective presence, all vary infinitely, according to the character of its abiding habits, according to the range of its experiences."——Ah! if we can grasp what this abiding means, if we can but touch even the hem of this truth, with the touch of faith, we have indeed come near to the border of the "good land." And, by the power of His life—"Christ in us"—we can thus approach, we can know, at last we will overcome, though now, fight we must. We can rest assured also, that no upward flight of holiness is too far a reach for us to seek: no victory over temptation too hard for us to attain, since with Christ for our Risen and Living Lord, "all things have become possible." Hence, if we do not overcome, it is not because His power fails, but because we hold back from full consecration of our all to Him. The consecration which He bids us seek and find when He calls us, saying: "I will bring you into the wilderness, and I will plead with you face to face."

Do you ask—Why call that a wilderness, which leads to Christ's converse with the soul intimate as the "pleading face to face"?

If you will recall His Gospel words, "Come unto Me, all ye that labor and are heavy laden, and I will give you rest," I think you will straightway see one reason. For they bear the same interpretation as this Old Testament invitation. And they bring out very plainly that the rest promised even when the soul is called near to Christ, is of a relative kind, for it springs from the fact, that His yoke is easy, and yet it is a burden—is a yoke only made easy by His sympathy and love; it brings out the fact, too, that our rest here is in comparison with earth's unrest, and that in bearing His yoke, even though He is with us, helping us bear it, we still, like the children of Israel, find there is no swift speeding across the desert to the "rest and inheritance," for our way there is like the path they trod, "a long way, round about."

Do you catch my idea? It is, that in the Gospel the call, "Come unto me .... I will give you Rest," is distinct from the following verses: the one, having to do with the "Hereafter," the others with now; the order being reversed from the Old Testament record, where first we encounter the thought of the wilderness, and afterward are granted the glimpse of the "promised land."

"Come unto Me." This is a call bidding us "leave the burden of mortal life, the sorrow of a sin-laden world, the weakness and the faulty character, the imperfect love of frail mortality; leave it all, and come—where? Not only to Heaven, not to your crown only, but to Me! and you shall find Rest, and that Rest shall be Heaven." We cannot, do not gain it here on earth, for the next verse tells us of the yoke and the burden, both involving continuance of labor and endurance, even though both are lightened by His Presence, and because of *that* Presence, while the discipline of life and temptation is a wilderness, "the desert is made to bloom," for "the beloved of the Lord shall dwell in safety by Him: and the Lord shall cover him all the day long."

If you spend an hour on the seashore you will understand this seeming contradiction of rest and unrest, for then you will see how, even amid the surging of the breaking waves, there is still a peaceful under-rippling current. Yes, dear, wonderful as it seems, if Christ's Presence be recognized by us, this under-ripple of peace is always ours, however the upper waves may dash and roar.—But—the abiding calm, unbroken by either ripple or wave, that, in its completeness we can only know when at last we are safe Home, at anchor, within the Harbor of Heaven.

I used the word crown, in referring to the Saviour's call to the soul, and it leads me to note in passing that there is danger of misreading the verse: "Be thou faithful unto death, and I will give thee a crown of life." For, if we merely see in the words the promise of a crown if we are faithful until death, they become discouraging, filling the heart with forebodings of failure, and the mind with thoughts of self, in place of the peaceful assurance of hope, that is a sure outcome of trust in Christ ; hence I do not think it was thus our Lord meant them, but rather as test words, asking, would our faithfulness be steadfast, and willing to endure suffering, even agony keen as death, for His sake? If we would, then they are His pledge of the blessed Hereafter which will be our crown of Life.

This is one of the many places where we walk in darkness if our faith only partially grasps the truth, that we only are complete *in* and *by* Him. But all is light if we depend on Christ for constant guidance, for then we do not try to bear alone the burden of being faithful, but we share it with Him, our Lord, who saves us not only from sin, but from its bondage.

The experiences I mention now may seem strange to you, for it is something of a contradiction, revealing that what is our greatest comfort may yet be our greatest humiliation.

It is that sometimes as we travel through this wilderness life, we become disheartened from the very fact of Christ's pleading with us "face to face." For it brings Him so near us, we see brought out in clearly-defined contrast our own unlikeness to the Divine Pattern. When it thus happens, remember, this very sight of the All-Perfect and our all imperfection is one of the wilderness ways, "to humble us, and to prove us"; for it shows what He is, and what we are, making our after conduct a test of whether we really are in profound earnest in wishing to be like Him.

But it is humbling, I repeat, dust humbling, this finding how dull and slow we are in responding to His example, and so is our wandering from Him. And yet, how we do wander, sometimes so far that where the light about us has been a clear shining, suddenly we find all dim, while a mist, caused by our waywardness and straying, gathers in thick gloom, like vapor up-rising from some sickly morass. And we cannot see our Lord at all: nevertheless He is near.

But the wanderer must pay the penalty of straying, and before we find our way back to the safe "narrow path," we may have to seek and seek, even till weary and footsore, the sun beating on us by day, the chill damp of night enfolding us with "a darkness that can be felt"—and then—for our humbling still—we find Him; find He has never left us—but we were the ones who turned from Him.

There are other times, when "our Lord hides His face," not because of any fault of ours, but for the perfecting of our faith, and that we may be fitted by His dealings for the object of them, the final receiving us "into glory." "Soldier and Servant"—it is a good motto for us wilderness-pilgrims, for we are called to fight the fight of faith, as well as to "walk in love, serving the Lord." And faith does oftentimes demand stern conflict, "the soul cannot satisfy itself with itself; it seeks some higher service. . . . And remember, faith will perish if we do not take care of it." It is not something we can plant in the soul, and then leave to grow. No, it needs the daily renewal of self-surrender, and daily seeking after the high service and devoted obedience of the children of God. If this is your desire, then listen to, and follow the "pleading" of "the sweet, low Voice that calls us out of ourselves, out of our vanities, out of our own ease, up to the higher obedience, up to the humility of sonship, up to the service of faith: that so nourishing and cherishing all the instincts that faith sets working within us, our faith may slowly perfect itself into that love of God which loves Him with all its mind, and all its heart, and all its soul, and all its strength."

And now, dear H——, you ask me to tell of the special "wilderness" you may be called to walk, living as you do a home and love-guarded life. It will doubtless be a wilderness leading into the realm of internal and spiritual temptations, rather than by the way of external and material. And yet, in meeting temptations, the same commands apply to both, though looking at them from a mere surface glance, it does not seem so. I recall once reading an illustration of this, which will serve to suggest the thought, though I cannot give it in the exact words used. The idea was in following the subtle working of temptation in its mental influence, take but the eighth commandment as an example, which holds good for a hundred other allurements : "Thou shalt not steal." Straightway you will say: "No need for me to pray to be delivered from that temptation, for never, in all my life, did I feel an impulse toward dishonesty."

But look a little deeper, and tell me, have you never been tempted to desire to seem a little better, a little truer, a little more charitable, a little more accomplished than you really are? Have you never given the impression of possessions or position a little beyond the honest truth? And—is not the being willing to seem anything which you are *not truly*, disobeying the command, "Thou shalt not steal"?—For, are you not trying to steal the good opinion of others, by giving them an impression of worth where it does not exist?

Alas, how often we do steal in one, if not all of these ways—and others, akin to them—without giving hardly a thought to the "moral falseness" involved—sometimes even smiling at our own rare skill in putting what the world calls the "best foot foremost."

Another of these subtle ways by which we are often tried is, we resist temptation because to yield would lower us in the estimation of others, not because of the right and wrong in question, and hence we gain nothing in a moral sense by our refusal; in fact, we lose in truth of character every time we *thus* conquer. For, while we may gain a certain strength toward resisting the evil when next it assails us, it is a mere surface gain, for "only as we refuse to yield because consent is sin in God's sight, do we really gain in spiritual strength, and power to close bar the door of our souls against future temptations."

Then, too, we are so wont to forget, that what we are to seek by the resisting of temptation is not deliverance from the penalty of wrong-doing, but from the *heart-sinfulness*, which leads us to desire to sin, making it even dear to us. How all this gives a profound emphasis to the truth, "the heart is deceitful."

Verily, victory over these subtle temptations, which, like all spiritual things, are difficult to grasp and hold, demands a keen intellectual effort, as well as prayerful seeking of Divine Help; this you will straightway see if you follow but the growth of one yielding. For it begins by a mental process, first the wish—and then the rounded thought—that reacts on the wish, pressing it forward, till desire gains mastery—and at last becomes a reality. Hence, to gain control over our wishes, is the way to gain control over thoughts, and when we have conquered so far as to hold sway over thoughts, we are well on toward that "great city, the Holy Jerusalem," of which it is written, "there shall in no wise enter into it anything that defileth .... or maketh a lie, but they which are written in the Lamb's Book of Life."

Truth, honesty of soul—yes, it leads by a path all upward, and if we tread its heights, even here on earth, we can look on and over into "the good land of promise."

> " O blest the land, the city blest,
> Where Christ the Ruler is confest!
> . . . . . .
> Fling wide the portals of your heart,
> Make it a temple set apart,
> From earthly use for Heaven's employ,
> Adorn'd with prayer, and love, and joy:
> So shall your Sovereign enter in,
> And new and nobler life begin.
>
> " Redeemer, come! I open wide
> My heart to Thee: here, Lord, *abide!*
> Let me Thy inner presence feel,
> Thy grace and love in me reveal,
> Thy Holy Spirit guide me on
> Until my glorious goal be won!"

But—before we reach that glad, blessed goal there are other wildernesses for us to encounter beside those typified by temptation—and those "other deserts" are so many, we will ponder them, dear H——, in a separate Meditation.

DESERT PLACES.

Remember,

"Our fathers did eat manna in the desert, as it is written, He gave them bread from Heaven to eat."
JOHN vi. 31.

And,

"Thus saith the Lord, I will make a way in the wilderness, and rivers in the desert."
Is. iv. 3.

And the Christ. He took them, His own chosen disciples—"into a desert place."
LUKE ix. 10.

IX.

DESERT PLACES.

YESTERDAY we pondered passing through the wilderness as a type of the soul's encounter with temptations in its journey through this world.

To-day, our thoughts lead to other experiences, that in their teaching of faith and patience, may well be called "desert places," and yet by knowing them, the heart is made ready for entrance at last into the King's own country—the dear Jerusalem the golden.

I need hardly tell you these deserts are varied as the clouds that speed between us and the blue sky, on an April day, when clouds above are well-nigh as many as the numberless waking flower-buds below, that spring up an hundred to a sod. For suffering is the appointed lot of all. And suffering! Who can count the ways by which it comes? Since they are so multitudinous, only the trials that stand out in boldest relief, will we pause to note. Chief among them is poverty—for when one must work whether the head be aching, or the heart breaking, it makes of labor a "desert place."

Ask the sons and daughters of toil, and they can tell you all about it. While as for sickness—truly it is a discipline that leads "apart into the desert." But, thank God, the desert of sickness is one of the places where we may feel most sure the Christ will come, filling its gloom with His Presence. The record of His life on earth gives us this assurance, for think of His tender sympathy for all bodily suffering. And surely the Lord Christ is no less tender and mindful than the Man Christ! Think how "they brought unto Him many that were sick": how we are told, not once, but again and again, "He was moved with compassion." And His compassion, what an example it is for us to follow, going as it did deeper than mere sympathy—precious as that is—for it was blended with the active mercy of relieving,—"the blind received their sight, and the lame walked, the lepers were cleansed, and the deaf heard."

From sickness our thoughts naturally pass on to the desert of parting. "One taken, the other left." Ah! that means a wilderness indeed; only they who have trod its desolate way know the barrenness of this "desert place."

And there is the desert of "living sorrows," the over-casting of a sun-bright sky, the turning of a flower-strewn path into the arid sand of the desert, because one we love has fallen from the ways of right to wrong, from honor to dishonor. Added to these trials are the numberless and the nameless anxieties and perplexities that belong to daily life. Conscience has dark places too, and remorse is a desert. And there are also the spiritual and mental deserts that follow swiftly on undue or self-conceited search into the "hidden things of God." But of them all the Lord saith, "I will make a way in the wilderness, and rivers in the desert." And yet, before He does this, the years of discipline my be long as the typical "forty"! For from His Word we learn that trial is meant to be trial, and that it must accomplish its full work. Christ said, "I am the true vine, and my Father is the husbandman: every branch in me that beareth not fruit He taketh away, and every branch that beareth fruit, He purgeth it that it may bring forth *more* fruit."

Remember it is not enough to be a branch, we must also "bear fruit." And then, "the Lord purgeth"—for the sake of the "*more* fruit." Hence we will have to cross and re-cross the deserts appointed for our discipline and growth in grace as long as we stay in this world. For there is no passing beyond tears, no passing beyond the need for weeping, till we are called *There*, where "God shall wipe away all tears."

Till then poverty will be hard in detail, sickness will mean weariness and pain, the parting from our dearest will be agony, the sin of those we love will be cruel as the wound of sharpest sword-blade. And yet, spite all this, God has a special comfort, as well as a special lesson linked with each trial, and He will reveal them to us when our hearts are ready for lesson and consolation.

Ah! if we only listen for His teaching in our keenest griefs, as well as in lesser trials, we will find they are in very truth "blessings in disguise." For, while the Lord saith, "I will cause you to pass under the Rod," a mercy is joined to that passing by a tie close as one brief connecting "*and*" "I will bring you into the bond of the covenant."

This being so, dear H——, our object is to seek how we may enter into this covenant bond though treading the preparatory deserts that help to perfect the soul for a Higher life. Let us take our place then as children under the schoolmaster law first, and then faith, for "the law *is* our schoolmaster to bring us unto Christ that we may be justified by faith." But, remember, "after that faith has come, we are no longer under a schoolmaster." What a blessed tender school it is by which we of this "new dispensation" are trained for the spiritual life. Since the coming of Christ and liberty, it stands out as something all unlike the bondage and rule of the old Mosaic law, as manhood is unlike infancy. Still, in a certain sense, these days are school days, but the order is reversed—law is still teacher, but Christ is the Higher Master, and in His school "*Love is Law—Law is Love.*" The difference turns for explanation to the continuous spiritual growth that has been going on ever since the world began. The history of a newly settled country will serve to straightway make my meaning plain. "In the early days law needed to be rigidly enforced, until habits and local customs had been founded; but when the claims of law had become firmly established, rule in many of its forms can safely be relaxed," just as in our hearts there is a time when we are governed by law. "I will obey, because I must," and the blessed aftertime when we act from the more noble principle of love and faith, which, while obedient to law, has passed beyond the need of its enforcement, though not beyond the need of the discipline of *love*.

And now let us strive to sum up a few of the lessons law and love teach.

You will remember in mentioning trials on the foregone page, poverty was the first I noted—and so we will first seek its lesson.

Canon Farrar writes: "Poverty, self-denial, the bearing of the yoke in youth, are the highest forms of discipline, for a pure and godly manhood." And he adds, "Humble poverty is true wealth." This exalts the being poor, but what does it teach?

In reply, let us turn again to Farrar; he says: "You have but little of this world's goods—oh, be faithful with that little, and you will find it more than much." *Faithfulness*, then, is one lesson we are to learn, and Farrar also tells us—"A poverty which scorns luxury, which can dispense with superfluities, which can find life purest and strongest when it is disciplined under the beneficent laws of 'high thinking and plain living' is wealthier in every element of happiness than

"'Forty seas, though all their shores were pearl,
Their waters crystal, and their rocks pure gold.'"

Another lesson obedience to law teaches is that, "whenever the labors of life are fulfilled in the spirit of striving against misrule, and doing whatever we have to do honorably and perfectly, however lowly the task, they invariably bring happiness." For, "ascending from the lowest to highest things, every scale of human industry worthily followed gives peace."—"Ask the laborer in the field, or at the forge, or in the mine; ask the patient, delicate-fingered artisan, or the strong-armed, fiery-hearted worker in bronze or in marble, and none of them who are true workmen will ever tell you that they have found the law of heaven an unkind one—that 'in the sweat of their brow they should eat bread until they return to the ground,' nor that they ever found it an unrewarded obedience, if indeed it was rendered faithfully to the command, 'Whatsoever thy hand findeth to do, do it with thy might.'" This is Ruskin's tribute to the blessing that is in even the poverty which enforces manual labor, and surely it proves while certain conditions will always make enforced daily toil a desert, yet it can become a wilderness wherein the "wayfaring man shall find an highway, and parched ground become a pool, and the thirsty land springs of water," if the laborer treads its path in obedience to the principle of doing with his might, rendering faithful hand and heart service.

These illustrations have all been taught by law. When we think of all love holds,

in promise of blessing and true riches for those who walk the desert of this world's poverty, we find enumeration save for a few beatitudes quite beyond our limits.——
"Blessed are the poor." That is our Saviour's halo for poverty—*blessed!*——" Let the poor glory in the beatitude of poverty, it is a gift of God." And for its peculiar trials, Christ's own tender solicitude provided. For, in anticipation of the sense of "aloneness," that often makes the hardest part of the trial of small means, He made Himself the companion of those who had but little of this world's wealth, and who are among its toilers. "Is not this the Carpenter? We may indeed be thankful that the word remains, for it is full of meaning, and has exercised a very noble and blessed influence over the fortunes of millions. It has tended to ennoble and sanctify the estate of poverty, to ennoble the duty of labor." And for the sake of doing this "Jesus Christ voluntarily chose the low estate of poverty, not indeed an absorbing, degrading, grinding poverty, which is always rare, and almost always remediable, but the commonest lot of honest poverty,

which though it necessitates self-denial can provide with care for all the necessaries of a simple life."

How love shines through all this—not the half-way love we mortals give, but love that manifests itself in the closeness of fellowship, sharing the yoke of poverty, bearing the burden of labor.

As for sickness—its law-taught lessons are so like an open page, I hardly need to sum them up, and yet we must not lose sight of these lessons, for when we have learned them, the desert of sickness, "that wilderness and solitary place shall be glad."

They are lessons that touch different notes of discipline; but the chief among them is, the learning submission in the acceptance of illness, in obedience to God's will. And then come like a troop of armed foes the special trials and temptations of illness. But, oh, the tenderness of this—love comes hand-in-hand with every trial and temptation, and we feel this love, when we cannot understand. For, "if we ponder on the incomprehensible nature of pain, mental and bodily, of its invisibleness, its vividness, its exceeding sharpness, and penetrating omnipresence in our whole being, of its inevitable origin, and the indissoluble link which binds it to sin : and lastly, its mysterious relation to the passion and perfection of our Lord, we shall see reason to believe, that a power so near and awful has many energies, and fulfils many designs in God's kingdom secret from us."

As for the many different kinds of pain that come through illness, one remedy holds good, and that is, bear them as bravely as you can—not being too eager to seek relief, for that is wont to lead to restlessness.

Bear as silently as possible too, and patiently, for *that* is always possible—and strive to remember—for this will be your greatest help—you are called to endure this physical trial, "as unto the Lord." And the burden does not rest on you alone, for He Himself "bore our sicknesses." " He, the Son of God, became what we are—God is with us in our flesh. . . . . He has that in His essential Godhead which need not be ashamed to call us brethren : as Love in a higher sense than we, He yet can embrace in His higher Sonship that lower sonship which is ours. He is made our Brother, our Brother-Man. All that is brotherly in nature—far more, all that is brotherly in man: all that reaches out hands to greet and welcome us, all sympathy that grows up, all encouragement that flows, all help that springs to meet our needs: all tenderness, all gentleness, all kindliness, all comfort, that soothes our misery: all pity, all compassion, all closeness of heart, all friendship, all love: all that comes to sweeten, to relieve, to support, to fortify: all courage to share, all unselfishness, all self-sacrifice, all this large brotherliness of man to man, is the work of the Son: all this is His prompting, His ministry, who for our sakes, since the children partake of flesh and blood, Himself partook of the same: He, the true Brother, Himself, in His own Person, came down and stood by our side, and shared all our ills, bore all our sicknesses, was bruised, was chastised: among us He came in our saddest need, and drank of our bitterest cup, and was baptized with our secret baptism that He might bring nigh to us all help, all comfort."—Oh, ponder it, dear H——, "He came, laying His hand upon our head in sickness, His fingers upon our eyes, sighing out His soul upon us, breathing His peace into us, touching us, taking us by the hand as we sink, entering into our homes, ... renewing us with the power of His love."

Yes, "there is nothing He will not share, nothing He will not comfort." He knows our pains, the measure and the number of them all, even to the bearing of weakness, which seems so slight a thing in comparison with acute suffering, and yet—how large a place it fills in sickness—what a desert weariness is!—It is a condition, too, as full of temptations as the branch of a thornbush is full of prickly thorns, and it brings its own tests and trials, their leaders, the impulse to selfishness, and self-indulgence. The only way to meet this phalanx of spiritual enemies that attack us through our weakness, is to fall back on the assurance that they come by God's will; they are sent as tests of our true and whole-hearted submission, and patient endurance is the work they demand from us. And if it leads to a place hard to cross as the weary stretch of a sandy desert—our Forerunner, Christ, knows all about it, and He will hear when we cry, "Have mercy upon me, O Lord, for I am weak." If you thus cry in profound earnest, even though the weary weakness does not leave your poor tired frame, you will nevertheless feel—"Though I am poor and needy, the Lord thinketh upon me."

And—the knowing, "He thinketh," it is a very restful pillow on which to fall back, and it changes the desert place "into the garden of the Lord."

And now, I will only briefly touch in passing, on the distressing forms of sickness which entail the loss of mental powers. If this trial comes to your beloved ones, all you can do is to seek shelter in the sure hope, though it may not be here on earth, yet God will in His own time fulfil His promise, and "the Holy Spirit will bring all things to remembrance." It is only for *now* that the light is dimmed—just for now, that the cloud is passing before the sun; *There* it will all come right, there will be no clouds—shadows will flee away.

In among the many lesser lessons illness teaches, I think perhaps one of the hardest to learn is the cheerful acceptance of one's separation from the home circle. Only they who have felt this, can estimate what it means to hear the faint sounds of dear family life—while memory follows its routine, the peaceful assembling for morning prayers, the gathering around the home-table, the familiar exchange of thought, and planning for the day's duties and pleasures—and one's self shut out from it all, by no barrier of distance save a closed door or dividing wall or two. This is no very great desert, I know—but it makes a stern demand on submissive patience. It is hard, too, to become reconciled to the fact that by God's will one is set to learn a different lesson from the dear loved ones of home—because life to an invalid is unlike life to the strong and well—nevertheless, this trial is linked with love—and love reveals new comforts and blessings—for there are "desert roses"!

As for "longings"—words cannot span the desert places they stretch over in an invalid's days. The longing for a sight of the blue sky, when one spends day after day in a darkened room—for a sight of God's fields and high hills—shady woods—a glimpse of a meadow and water-brooks—or even for a clump of wild-flowers growing by the road-side. There come hours, too, when longings crave for still wider out-looks—mountains and broad flowing rivers—great lakes—and the sea—the wide, free, beautiful sea!—Oh, how we long for them—only the "sick and weary" know. But, they are the only ones who know, too, "how many of our best things we learn in sickness." I copy that sentence from one who penned a leaflet called the "Illuminated Valley"—and close following it, this servant of God wrote: "To me it is a new school of theology, or rather the higher and more illustrative department of the old. I did not know how strong the arms are which Christ puts around His sick and suffering disciples until I felt myself sinking into them for support; how tender the bosom of the Infinite Love, till there was nothing else for me to lean upon."

Surely such an experience is worth the enduring of many longings; and there are many more than these few which I have enumerated, not the least among them a desire for independence that comes with the wish for a bit of free motion, even if it be nought more than the crossing a room, the being able to stand before a friendly bookcase choosing one's own volume.

Well—what profit comes of all these trials? Growth in grace God grant—grace to leave all longing—all restlessness—with Him: knowing He will satisfy them if it be best for us; knowing, too, and this is a flower of the obedience of faith, that had any other way been equally good for us, God would have trained by it. Hence, our part is not to question, but to obey—even if the command be only to "lie still."

Before leaving this subject you ask me, dear H——, to give you one word revealing *love* in those subtle and trying sicknesses that rank under the name of "nervous diseases."

I remember reading in a volume of comfort for invalids—a book written, I think, by the sister of Frederick Maurice—a passage that, I trust, will come to you like the touch of a soothing hand when next you are troubled by nervous suffering. "Do not struggle, for it increases nervous troubles fearfully—just lie still. He is love, and very pitiful, and of tender mercy. Surely, then, He is grieved with and for you—is 'touched with a feeling of your infirmities'—for 'He was in all points tempted like as we are, yet without sin.' He bore nervous sufferings. How intensely He must have entered into them; every nerve of His was pierced, and wounded, and stretched. Say then, 'O Saviour of the world, who by Thy cross and precious blood hast redeemed us, save us, and help us, we humbly beseech Thee, O Lord.' 'Fear not: He *will* strengthen you, and uphold you by the right hand of His righteousness.'"

I would fain linger over still other desert places to which illness leads, but space forbids. I would fain, too, give you a word of cheer for the wearisome nights appointed, the sleepless hours when you say, "Would God it were morning," and yet the morning tarries. Yes—I would fain give you a word of cheer—and lo! I have done it, for remember that word "*appointed.*" God knows and God rules. What a light that knowledge sends gleaming across the darkness and the weariness—in its beams, spite the tossing and restlessness, you know the "Everlasting Arms *are* underneath," for He has promised to "make all your bed in sickness."

But how when the day comes, and you meet the ever-recurring "What can I do? Must I lie useless hour after hour?"—

A great help in answering that question is to remember you are only commanded to do what God gives you strength for, and in the matter of "effort" there is always as much danger of sinning by overdoing as by underdoing! Then, too, you have a work, for there is always the learning of patience.

But we must leave illness and its teachings where "law and love" are so closely interblended. Enough if we have learned its great lesson is obedience, for then we will find help in our striving to attain it, from the knowledge that, "though He was a Son, yet learned He obedience by the things which He suffered." And if we, too, are called to suffer, "it is the will of God," and if cheerfully borne, because His will, we will find when we "have passed through all that great and terrible wilderness," emblemed by suffering and sickness, then "we will come unto the mountain . . . . which the Lord our God doth give us."

What a blessed sequel to our wilderness journey! Think of the seeing, the longings satisfied, when we look up and off from the Mountain Height to which the discipline of our pilgrim days has led!

It will be worth all it costs—all—

> "To rest in trust: O German hymn,
> Fill all my heart—my faith is dim!

> "To leave with Thee: in Thy dear hand
> All things I cannot understand.
> To rest in trust: O German hymn,
> Fill all my soul—my faith is dim!

> "To ask Thee not the when or how,
> With yielded heart to only bow;
> To find the joy that comes at length
> From leaning sweetly on Thy strength.

> "To be Thy child: so, lying still,
> To rest in trusting on Thy will;
> No other arm can fold away
> So tenderly from night till day!

> "To take the peace He daily giveth
> Unto each troubled heart that liveth;
> However weak to find my share
> Of the dear Shepherd's gentle care.

> "O rest of trust! O trust in rest!
> Sweet German hymn, thy faith is blest."

One thing remains for me to add to this long meditation; and that is not an easy thing to explain. It is the lesson held in prosperity. The Old Testament record is a beacon-light pointing to this truth. "He found him in a desert land, and in the waste howling wilderness. He led him about, He instructed him. . . . He made him ride on the high places of the earth, that he might eat the increase of the fields; and He made him to suck honey out of the rock, and oil out of the flinty rock." "But" (oh, heed this warning if you are called to meet the test of prosperity), after it all, "Jeshurun forsook God who made him, and lightly esteemed the Rock of His Salvation. . . . And when the Lord saw it He said, I will hide my face."

Sad as it is, this lack of gratitude—even amounting to the forsaking the Lord—is wont to be now, as it was then, the afterpart of great success in the things of this world. It makes one tremble at the very thought of great possessions, for our Lord Christ said: 'How hardly shall they which have riches enter the kingdom of Heaven."——

You will remember, in numbering "deserts," the parting from our dear ones filled a foremost place, as it does in reality—but when called to that wilderness "consider in thine heart, that as a man chasteneth his son, so the Lord thy God chasteneth thee." . . . . And the promise is—even by that way of the desert of loneliness, you will be brought—if you keep "the commandments of the Lord," to "a good land—a land of brooks of water, of fountains, and depths that spring out of valleys and hills." Yes, if we yield our will to God's will—and calmly, bravely, cheerfully, tread the path He appoints—all these "desert places" we have pondered will guide to the "land of wheat and barley, and vines and fig-trees, and pomegranates: a land of oil olive and honey—a land wherein thou shalt eat bread without scarceness, thou shalt not lack anything in it: a land whose stones are iron, and out of whose hills thou mayest dig brass."

Dear—with such a prospect—such a hope—I repeat—is not the discipline life brings us worth all it costs?

Think, these verses are types—every one

rich with a spiritual as well as a material significance; for in the Bible, metaphor is the warp and woof of language. Hence the "*wheat*" stands as an emblem of vitality—grains of wheat, as we know, having been locked in mummy-cases for thousands of years, yet retaining the germ of life, which springs up when they are planted in the kindly earth. "*Olive oil,*" you know how it is identified with "thoughts of peace, forgiveness, and charity"—the "*Vine*" with "wisdom and intelligence," and the deeper, dearer, more sacred meanings which the Gospel entwines about it. The "*Iron*" and "*Brass,*" too, what well-known types they suggest of character. In truth there is not one of the terms used in these verses but it is full of significance—a sort of word-picture.——

But to return to the "desert of parting"—death here, leading to Life There—before we ponder it we will pass on, and find its comfort in meditating on "Open Windows." —Yes, we will go to the sepulchre, and God grant we may find the "stone rolled back from the door."

OPEN WINDOWS.

"Prove me now herewith, saith the Lord of Hosts, if I will not open you the windows of Heaven, and pour you out a blessing."
MALACHI iii. 10.

Remember:

"God illumines those who think often of Him, and lift their eyes toward Him."
JOUBERT.

"This one thing I do, forgetting those things which are behind, and reaching forth unto those things which are before, I press toward the mark for the prize of the high calling of God in Christ Jesus."
PHIL. iii. 13-14.

X.

OPEN WINDOWS.

AS children seek flowers when spring comes, spreading its mantle of bloom over all the land, so let us to-day, dear H——, go forth and look for the Windows that open Heavenward.

Verily, I think we will find them unveiled for faith's eye to scan their farthest reach, and our beholdings will be as varied as the blossoms that star hill-side and meadow, shady nook and sunny field, when April glides into May, and May speeds on to June. For, truly, words are too narrow to span the comforts that come in-flooding the soul with light, even at darkest hours, in response to the earnest cry: "Thou art my lamp, O Lord; lighten my darkness."

But this illumining of dark places will not come all at once. No, spiritual sight is too progressive for that, hence the emblem of sunrise so often applied to its expanding, increasing radiance. You know the way of sunrise—first the gray dawn, the break of day, and then a kindling glow on the highest mountain peaks—a glow that descends in ever growing brightness from hill-top to hill-top, till at last the remotest lowland valley catches a reflection of the glory, and all the world is bathed in the radiance of God's daily repeated command, "Let there be light." This is nature's story, and the soul's history repeats it, save for the fact that full radiance is not our portion here, for *that* we must wait till earth is exchanged for Heaven, for here always there will be an horizon-line to shut us in. Nevertheless we will seek the windows that are open—beginning by the suggestions of comfort and support—which in-shine in consolation beams for the hour we all must meet—the hour when "death comes up into our windows."

As we ponder this great mystery—mortal death as the birth of immortal life—we will use the word in its common acceptation. I know there are those who look forward to it as a glad prospect, those who long for its coming, whose faith is so clear shining, death is by them anticipated with no more dread than "the passing from one room into another." But you tell me, dear H——, you are not one of those thus blessed with a "willingness to depart." You tell me you fear dying, and I think there is nothing wrong in your feeling; certain I am it is the most universal way of regarding departure. And it is but natural that the human heart should shrink before the profound mystery of the silence which no voice has ever yet broken—from which none have ever yet come back to tell us the way it leads. Yes, it is all strange, unknown, and its inevitableness, its exceeding vagueness, its exceeding loneliness of familiar companionship, all combine to fill the heart with trembling awe; and I repeat, surely this is not wrong, for nothing in Holy Scripture indicates that God condemns it—on the contrary, much goes to prove that our Lord Himself regarded it as a crucial test for the timid faith of His followers.

Hence He has richly strewn the pages of the Old and New Testaments with promises of Divine help, providing a full store of dying grace for the dying hour. But we need not be discouraged because we cannot grasp that grace in advance, for it will surely be granted us with the need for it—then all will be well; and what we have to do now is "to trust that the love which has met the needs of busy life many a time with unexpected and surprising adaptations, will, when the time comes, and the necessity is close at hand, give the needed grace to die." And now let us gather up and meditate on the repeated assurances of our Saviour's nearness, which can illumine the dying hour with the light of Life Eternal. Think of His strength-giving promises—"Fear not, I will be with thee." "Lo! I am with you alway." You shall be "delivered from the burden of the flesh"; "corruption shall put on incorruption"; "mortality shall put on immortality"; "you shall obtain joy and gladness"; "sorrow and sighing shall flee away"; and "God shall wipe away all tears from your eyes: and there shall be no more death, neither sorrow, nor crying, neither shall there be any more pain." Tell me, do not these thoughts open a window toward Heaven

—its out-look all peace? Surely they are given to help us on our way Thitherward, and yet, how solemn a thing it is to remember, our thoughts of Heaven are wont to correspond to our spiritual life. If you look deep into your own heart you will know this, and you will have a sight of the real Heaven for which you long. "Examine that, and it will show you precisely your spiritual position, just as the traveller knows his latitude by looking at the north star, and noting its distance above the horizon. What are the aspirations that go up from the profound within you? What sort of a world would you make for yourself, if you could have everything your own way, and embody around you your own best imaginations? Answer this question honestly, and your idea of Heaven is defined to you, and you will see whether it be carnal and selfish, or spiritual and pure." I have wandered from your saying that there are other reasons beside the physical dread of dying, and the mystery of going out into the unknown that make you dread death. You tell me, there is the consciousness of sin, not only of the great omissions and commissions that, like darksome caverns, fill so many places in the record of your life—but the vast concourse, too, of what may be called "lesser faults" ill-temper, wrong thoughts, idle dreams, the half-wayness of repentance, the little love and praise, little real devotion you have rendered your Lord, languid prayers, dull meditations—all these voices of conscience come flooding your memory, and making your heart tremble, for all the while you knew the right and yet you chose the wrong.

Yes, dear—and so it is with us all; hence, no wonder the heart fails when we come to know our life's book is written full; the last page turned, the last step taken, there is no time left to retrace even so much as one line, no time for struggle with, and victory over temptation, for we must go, just as we are.

But this is only looking at one side; turn to the other and all is changed in a moment from darkness to light, from despair to hope; for, there is one thing left we can do—we can cling to the Crucified! Cling so close to His cross that in its shadow we will lose self and sin, giving *all* into His care, and He is so willing to take it—so willing.——Then be not faithless, but believing—for neither death nor life can separate us from His boundless Love.—Oh! the window that Love opens for us—one look through its wide-flung curtain reveals enough to take fear away; for it shows us that He, the Christ, knows all about dying, knows even the agony of feeling the weight of sin; for though He was all sinless, for our sake He carried the burden of sin, and thus from us the load is taken. He knows, too, all the weariness and physical weakness and languor of dying. He passed through its vagueness and mystery that He might say to us, "Fear not"—for remember, "When from the Cross sounded His Voice, proclaiming, 'It is finished,' it meant the deepest darkness of death was finished for each of His followers. Henceforth not one would ever have to pass through it alone." Oh, believe this, and "let not your heart be troubled, neither let it be afraid."

As for the time and manner of our departure, let us seek to have no will of our own —it is so much the more peaceful way—and about dying, as about suffering, it is true,

> "The law of pain is Love alone,
> The wounding is to heal."

We can safely trust and leave all with Him, who "has appointed a set time"—and who will, when that time comes, remember us, and be very near us—for "I have graven thee on the palms of my hands, saith the Lord."

Faber's hymn, "Wishes about Death," is so full, so fragrant with the restful calm, the quietness and confidence of leaving all to Christ, and yet being true to self in natural desire, thinking you may not know it, I will copy it for you, verse by verse:

> "I wish to have no wishes left,
> But to leave all to Thee:
> And yet I wish that Thou shouldst wish
> Things that I wish should be.
>
> "And these two wills I feel within
> When on my death I muse:
> But, Lord, I have a death to *die*,
> And not a death to choose.
>
> "Why should I choose? for in Thy love
> Most surely I descry
> A gentler death than I myself
> Should dare to ask to die.

"But Thou wilt not disdain to hear
    What these few wishes are
Which I abandon to Thy love,
    And to Thy wiser care.

"Triumphant death I would not ask,
    Rather would deprecate:
For dying souls deceive themselves
    Soonest when most elate.

"All graces I would crave to have
    Calmly absorbed in one—
A perfect sorrow for my sins,
    And duties left undone.

"I would the light of reason, Lord,
    Up to the last might shine,
That my own hands might hold my soul
    Until it passed to Thine.

"And I would pass in silence, Lord,
    No brave words on my lips,
Lest pride should cloud my soul, and I
    Should die in the eclipse.

"But when and where, and by what pain,—
    All this is one to me;
I only long for such a death
    As most shall honor Thee.

"Long life dismays me, by the sense
    Of my own weakness scared;
And by Thy grace a sudden death
    Need not be unprepared.

> "One wish is hard to be unwished—
> That I at last might die
> Of grief, for having wronged with sin
> Thy spotless Majesty."

What!—after all this—do you again tell me you fear "because you are a sinner"?— Dear, did I not tell you He has bidden us leave ourselves with Him?—and sin is a part of self.

But you say, "the wages of sin is death." Yes—but His Love in its fulness of forgiveness and redemption has paid those wages for us—it is Love like an ocean; fathomless to any plummet ever yet discovered by the wisest man this world has known. Can you not trust that Love? Can you not believe in victory over sin through our Lord Jesus Christ? Try to remember, "He hath overcome the sharpness of death, and opened the kingdom of Heaven for all believers"; thus the question is—not the magnitude of your sinfulness—but—do you believe?— "He hath opened the kingdom of Heaven." What a window this promise, through which comes the in-shining brightness of the Sun of Righteousness.

Think of the "kingdom of Heaven," and

what it means—and remember, in Christ's use of the words the light falls from above down on to our daily life, for they are linked with a thought of service here below.

Yes—the kingdom of Heaven belongs to *now* as truly as to the blessed Hereafter.

You will catch my meaning, if you repeat the Lord's prayer—" Thy will be done, ... Thy kingdom come on earth as in Heaven "—for this is a petition that asks not for flight into the Heaven above, but for entrance into Heaven here and now—the spiritual Heaven whose realm is in the soul, and of which Christ tells us, saying—" Verily I say unto you, except ye be converted and become as little children, ye shall not enter into the kingdom of Heaven ; whosoever therefore shall humble himself as a little child, the same is greatest in the kingdom of Heaven." Hence, what we have to seek is child-likeness of spirit, and that we may know what that is, windows of interpretation are set wide open on every side ; dull indeed must we be to miss their meaning, and yet we need to be careful lest we over-look the difference Scripture so plainly notes between childishness and child-likeness. You know the characteristics of a childish soul—self-confidence, selfishness, lack of stability, fretfulness, waywardness; and you know, too, how unlike they are to the child-likeness which is marked by trustfulness, submission, and the sweet simplicity of a heart pure in thought and intent. And to have a soul full as a garden of flowers with such sweet traits, is to have the kingdom of Heaven within, and we may have it—no matter how far, according to time's counting of years, we have passed beyond the limits of childhood, for to souls there is no such thing as old age; return to the true spirit of child-likeness is always possible—and by thus returning we come into harmony with the law of growth, for childhood is a type of growth,—— and then—think of the sequel to all this!— When growth has come to the limit God sets for each soul to attain through the discipline of life, then we pass on to that Higher Heaven where the soul's language will ever be the child's "Abba, Father."

For child-likeness does not end here, it is so truly a part of the ever abiding "Faith, Hope, and Love," which reach on and on beyond our power to follow, for "eye hath not seen, nor ear heard, neither hath it entered into the heart of man to conceive, the things which God hath prepared for them that love Him."

All this leads us round again, to the promise, "He hath opened the kingdom of Heaven"; but now, we seek not the in-ward, but the on-ward looks which take us close to the Border-land of the Heavenly Country, where there is no more dying. Knowing this, surely we need not fear either to let our dearest go, or to go ourselves in response to the call bidding us leave this world for the next—for—He who thus calls is the One "who has tasted death for every man"— He, whose name is Jesus, and "He shall save His people from the power of the grave." Remember, He has promised to be "the strength of your heart," and "His strength is made perfect in weakness." Death here is a mere gate leading to Life There—for, "Except a corn of wheat fall into the ground and die, it abideth alone; but if it die, it bringeth forth much fruit." How the emblem truth of that verse is all aglow with life—kindling the dying here with beams of radiance from the living There. And, of these beams of light that fall aslant the Hereafter the Bible is so full. If you will but read it with a mind wide awake to find the passages which make immortality real, I think your heart will be filled with gladness, and with wonder, too, at the openings Heavenward—for, truly, "the windows of Heaven do open," and in the hope of all they reveal, how the Future broadens! And silence, too, grows full of music, for we begin to know what the words mean which tell, "you shall come to Zion with songs and everlasting joy." Only have faith—then the promise is so sure, "ye shall obtain"—even as they, our dear ones, have obtained entrance into the Heavenly Home—for, while there is much veiling of the "Other Shore," Christ's own words assure us they who have heard His call, and gone, are at Rest now, safe Home—with Him—for His prayer was—"Father, I will that those whom Thou hast given Me, be *with Me, where* I am."

Truly there is no love like the love of Jesus—no solace so tender as the comfort He gives, when He lets us gaze through the window that opens toward the "green pastures and the still waters" of the land into which our beloved have entered. Only they who have held the hand of the precious departing one, till verily they have let it go, because Christ's Hand has led within, can know the full, sacred, holy meaning that haloes the death of His Saints.

Such in-looks belong to the glorious liberty and light of the children of God, for by them we behold with the eye of faith "the Heavens open and the Son of Man, Jesus our Mediator, sitting on the right hand of God"— and where He is, they are— our dearest— His Saints! When in the night of sorrow God grants us such an onward look, it is as when a storm suddenly clears away, and stars shine through the rifts in the clouds; and then we know, too, what it means to hear "songs in the night." —That is the Old Testament promise of consolation. And the New echoes it in the words, "sorrowing yet rejoicing."

Ponder for a moment those promised songs, and remember they are not blossoms out of sunshine, like flowers, but they are night songs, born out of sorrow, of which darkness stands as the type; and yet, though we learn them through trouble, they are full of the music of comfort, *for*, "God giveth them."—"The God, who is our refuge and our strength, a very present help in trouble."—"The God of all comfort, who comforteth us in all our tribulations." And because of this comfort we "glory in tribulation," we can even sing, for "the Lord is good, a stronghold in the day of trouble: and—He knoweth them that trust Him." He has promised, "as one whom his mother comforteth, *so* will I comfort you." In "His love and His pity He will redeem." And, you will find, as life goes on, that "the Gethsemane places have done more for you than the Mount of Transfiguration"—and that "God's comforts are always greater than our troubles."

It is, too, by acquiescing in God's will we learn to thankfully—yes, thankfully—accept trouble, since He permits it, and thankfulness is another word for song—and "every sorrow brings a peace with it."

How can your heart enter into harmony with this? I know but one reply to give you—and that is, do not seek for the songs or the peace, *but* seek Him who giveth them, and they will be the outcome of His felt Presence in the soul, as sure as sunrise is the outcome of day-dawn. This is how we Christians live "sorrowing yet rejoicing lives," and the turning to Him in our midnight grief is like passing from darkness to light—hence the songs come unbidden, not because we seek them, I repeat, but because we seek the God who gives them. When He thus fills the soul, then, as at the coming of the morning, the birds of the air break forth with song, so our hearts sing; and the simpler, the fuller our trust in Christ, the fuller and sweeter the songs. This leads me to repeat what I said in a former meditation—hence we do not welcome suffering for what *it is*, but for what *it does!*—and nothing is so wont to lead *near* to God as sorrow. And now your next query is, "How can you find windows of Heaven opening?" My reply must again seem a repetition, for all I can tell you is—not by seeking them through the experience of others—for God gives to each one of us a special revelation, and we can only come to that revelation by accepting the conditions of our surroundings, and doing our duty in them faithfully and trustfully; and—you will forgive the warning—this is a place where there is always danger of giving "an undue prominence to the blessed and glorious work that has been done for us without us, to the exclusion of the equally blessed and all-important work which must be accomplished within us before we can be meet for the Heavenly inheritance that has been purchased for us, and to which we can have no possible claim but the unmerited mercy of Jesus Christ." This being so, the fullest answer I can give to your query of how to obtain Heavenward glimpses, is the simple reply, live near to the Source of Light; for the closer we keep to that Light, the more we see; dark places grow so plain in its illumining; mists so vanish before its shining. Yes, wonderful as it is, if we live near Christ, like Stephen of old, we may see the "Heavens opened." But, for such a blessed seeing, we must have Stephen's spirit, we must look "steadfastly up into Heaven."

Another window of Comfort that Christ has opened wide for us, is the blessed sureness we have through His death and resurrection—which is the pledge of ours—that we will meet our dear ones in Heaven. Only for *now* is the parting. Among the Bible records that serve to make this most sure, how clearly defined against the blue sky of the Gospel narrative is the appearing of Moses and Elias on the Transfiguration Mount—where we are told "they talked of the Lord's decease, which He should accomplish at Jerusalem." What a token this, that while our eyes are holden from the joy of seeing our beloved, they may yet see us—and have knowledge to some extent of what is going on here on earth—and of what is to be our future. Think, too, of the glimpse that record gives of the resurrection of the body—for they both "heard" and "spoke."

This leads us to the window widest open of all, for through it shines that most blessed assurance of Life Hereafter, which is revealed by Christ's words: "I am He that liveth." Liveth!—that is a promise of perpetual life: there is no echo of death in it. And it is a life which reaches out and enfolds every one of us—stamping with permanency all love that is "love in Christ."

This makes friendship such a blessed lasting thing, with no break in its real linking of heart to heart, even though for a time we be separated—the one from the other. A lasting thing, I repeat, lasting beyond our *now* power of conception—for who can span eternity by a thought?—Who can limit the growth of an endless affection? And the deeper and fuller the heart we love, the surer we become of this truth of love's immortality, for it is the most earnest souls that bear the richest testimony that this life is not all. And, as though to make this even more certain, we have but to look from the heart of friendship on to the revelations made plain by the life of Christ, for there we see Love triumphing over mortal death, as truly as Life triumphs over the grave. If for a time, in the first agony of the wrench of parting from our dearest, we cry out in doubt of this—"Lord, tell me, will we meet again?"—softly as the dew falls on flowers in the gloom of midnight darkness, we hear in reply, the tender whisper of the "Still, Small Voice"—"Thy brother *shall* live again!" And—the crown to that promise, you know it—for "Christ has Risen!" and His empty tomb has become the pledge to us that the grave does not hold the dear souls of those gone before us, who, through His redemption and resurrection "are not dead, but alive forevermore."

How like a warm hand-clasp of comfort for the deepest depth of grief comes this knowledge, even though it leads us to the sepulchre in the garden. A place where we need to tread very softly, for it is holy ground—so holy, much of silence and mystery veils it. Nevertheless, since the dawning of the Resurrection day, though it be a path leading by the way of graves, we know it is "God's acre," and its onward is the "Many-Mansioned Home," of which Christ said, "I go to prepare a place for you." For, though graves have been no less since that day, they are no longer tight-sealed and stone-guarded. No—when the stone was rolled from our Saviour's tomb, henceforth stones were rolled from all graves, whatever be the sorrow they mark, and onlooks were granted beyond the "dying and the weeping."

Such wonderful on-looks—for so tender

is the Saviour's pity for us, He even "maketh intercession," that these looks may penetrate on to the blessedness of which He says, "that they may behold my glory." And, "because the Father loves, the Son's prayer of Love is granted." For *Love* is the other side of the grave!

Remember when sorrow comes — that other side — *Love, and Home!* — I often wonder what we would do amid the fragmentary, broken places of this uncertain existence which is at best

> " A wave, a shadow, a breath, a strife,
> With change and change forever rife."

How we could bear it, were it not that the Hope given by "Him who was dead and now liveth forevermore" bridges over our uncertainty, and is planted firm within the golden gate through which we will "for Christ's sake" pass at last.

Yes, dear H——, for you and for me the gates will open, though now they seem so close shut; we may — wonderful thought — even this very hour stand within their enclosure; we may be "nearer Home," — "nearer now than we think."

You ask me, before we leave this subject, to look with you through "the window of prayer"—and you prelude your request by the question, "What is prayer?" Old Bunyan's definition is, "Prayer is the pitcher that fetches water from the brook." If this be so, surely a window is open in Heaven from which light descends to make clear the reflections mirrored in the "brook in the way," whose waters are replenished by the prayers of God's pleading children.

A full gleam of radiance shines, too, on the spirit of submission, which is the key-note of true prayer. For if we follow our "great Exemplar in Prayer" we must say, "Thy will, not mine, be done." Perseverance is another bright shining wavelet; and here, also, we have our Lord's example—for He offered one prayer three times, and surely we learn from His frequent resorting to the refuge of prayer that it is the best preparation for trial. But the dearest place to which the thought of our praying Lord leads, is the example He gives that we may plead for our precious ones, even as He prayed for His own. "What a blessing, too, is the spiritual telegraphy of prayer! We never pray alone, but encircled by those whose wants are dear to us, and our prayers are buoyed up by the wants and aspirations of those who mingle in them. It is such a privilege to thus go to God with the importance which linking others' wants to ours gives to our petitions." What out-reaching that extract suggests!—Let us look at prayer, too, from a backward view, and recall how "the practice of prayer is co-extensive with the idea of religion"; for "wherever man has believed a higher power to exist, he has not merely discussed the possibility of entering into converse with such a power: he has assumed as a matter of course that he can do so." "Sacrifice begins at the very gate of Eden. The life of early Patriarchs is described as a 'walking with God'—a continuous reference of thought and aspiration to the Father above." How this early-felt need of communion through prayer points on to the time when "the new revelation was made in Jesus Christ," and when "there was little to add to what was already believed as to the power and obligation of prayer beyond revealing the secret of its acceptance." Think, too, of our Lord's precepts and example; they are sufficiently emphatic. And His apostles appear to represent prayer not so much as a practice of the Christian life as its very truth and instinctive movement. The Christian must be "continuing instant in prayer"; he must "pray without ceasing." One word more from this author's thoughts, and I think you will call the window of prayer wide open. It is—remember, "prayer is emphatically religion in action. It is the soul of man engaged in that particular form of activity which presupposes the existence of a great bond between itself and God. Prayer is, therefore, nothing else or less than the noblest kind of human exertion. It is the one department of action in which man realizes the highest privilege and capacity of his being. And, in doing this, he is himself enriched and ennobled almost indefinitely: now, as of old, when he comes down from the mountain his face bears tokens of an irradiation which is not of this world."

We have dwelt much in this little diary on the lesson of "sorrow" and of "service"

—and yet you ask me, before we come to its last page, to point you to still another window through which you may view them both by gazing Heavenward. In reply, for "sorrow," I copy words from Robertson, for they flood with light to my mind, and I think will to yours, the truth that sorrow's mission is the development of a higher spiritual life. "Sorrow is not an accident, occurring now and then; it is the very woof which is woven into the warp of life. God has created the nerves to agonize and the heart to bleed; and before a man dies, almost every nerve has thrilled with pain and every affection has been wounded. The account of life which represents it as probative is inadequate: so is that which regards it chiefly as a system of rewards and punishments. The truest account of this mysterious existence seems to be that it is intended for the development of the soul's life, for which sorrow is indispensable. Every son of man, who would attain the true end of his being, must be baptized with fire. It is the law of our humanity, as that of Christ, that we must be perfected through suffering. And he who has not discerned the divine sacredness of sorrow, and the profound meaning which is concealed in pain, has yet to learn what life is. The cross, manifested as the necessity of the highest life, alone interprets it."

As for the window that looks toward the prophecy held in service, it is not far to seek—for, as indolence is always like a moth in its subtle but sure destruction of energy, steadfast earnest service is a correspondingly sure indication of advance; and all advance in the spiritual life is an open window showing as its sign that the same mighty conqueror who was victorious over the grave, will be triumphant in the overcoming of spiritual death in our souls if we earnestly seek to serve Him.

And service is something with which *all* life is hedged in, since it can be rendered by a passive obedience as well as active—and though "it is by active performance of service for others, that self is most wont to be cast out of sight, and unselfish love to our neighbor expanded," yet quiet and seemingly uneventful lives offer plenty of opportunities for this, too. For, there is always the conflict with sins around us, and within, and I know no better way of pointing toward the window that struggle with temptation opens, than that which Farrar tells—when he writes: "He who tempers the wind to the shorn Lamb, tempers also the temptations to the weak soul.

"He knoweth our frame, He remembereth that we are but dust. Oh, in that hero-multitude who follow the Lamb whithersoever He goeth, think not that there are only the dauntless, and the powerful, the great in heart and the strong in faith: no, there are many of the weak and timid, many of the obscure and the ignorant, many of the shrinking and the suffering there. We saw not, till they were unfolded for the flight of death, the angel wings."

The window through which weariness looks Heavenward!—its prospect is all Rest—that blessed rest they know, who serve Him day and night with never a need to say —"I am tired."—

And, now, we will take just one glance through the window Paul throws so wide for all believers, when he writes: "This one thing I do, forgetting those things which are behind, and reaching forth unto those things that are before, I press toward the mark for the prize of the high calling in Christ Jesus."

Words, these, that portray the heritage that only belongs to the Christian! even the right to forget the past—and in that forgetting we find a window opening toward the future that is verily as full of promise as the bud is the promise of fruit.

But remember, there is but one way given by which we are enabled to forget—and that is, by reaching forward; for the object of each experience is the fitting the soul for another, while the thing we accomplish is always of so much less importance in God's sight, than what we become through its developing power.

This constant progress, constant "stepping-Heavenward," is so the mark of true soul life, for the command, "Speak unto the children of Israel that they go forward," is as much a command for us now, as it was for God's children of old; and just as they had nothing to do with the land of bondage after they had passed its confines, so we have nothing to do with our *past* when we have given our hearts to Christ, for we gave *that* to Him, too—and, spite the sins that stain its record—He has promised, "sins shall be blotted out, remembered no more," hence they are not for us to recall. And, certainly, with whatever of good there may have been in our by-gone, we have nothing to do—He will take care of it—our path is all forward!

I think this is why such a deep significance is given in the Bible to "looking back"—and why the emblem of death is set as a warning against it. You remember Lot's wife dead—dead—only in punishment for a backward look!—No wonder this solemn lesson has stood a type of spiritual death, through the ages that have come and gone since the angel voice proclaimed— " Escape for thy life, look not behind thee, ... escape to the mountains."

Do you ask, what I think the prize Paul sought—and which, in following his example, we are to seek?

Likeness to Christ, is my reply; thus it is always something beyond us, for the more like Him we become, the fuller and deeper is our knowledge of what He is, and the more eager grows our reaching forth after likeness to Him. Yes—surely this was the prize Paul desired—for it was not Heaven he sought, Heaven was in his heart already. It was not to be saved—for of salvation he was already assured through the love of Christ—hence, plainly, we see it was likeness to the great Example.

And with such a prize set before him, how could he help "counting all things but loss that he might win"? Ah! well might he term it "a high calling." And lest we be discouraged as we strive to run this race, not *perfection*, but *faithfulness* is made the test of success; while being perfect is always the open window toward which faithfulness points, granting us through it, even now, glimpses of the blessed hereafter, when we shall "wake up in His likeness": when we shall enter within "the veil whither the forerunner—Jesus—is already entered for us."

And so, dear H——, all we have to do is to run with patience "the race set before us, looking unto Jesus, the author and finisher of our faith." And not looking for what the world calls success—for that our Lord never promised us in this life. No, He said—"In the world ye shall have tribulation." Nevertheless, He bade us "be of good cheer." Hence this is a command that we must read in the same way that we look at a rough transparency, whose inequalities reveal naught but a broken surface as we gaze down on it, but which, when held up for the light to illume, becomes a beautiful picture; just as tribulations held up toward the light become transparent and full of Love's revealing. And those rays of Light—remember, they are to be on-reaching, even to the including others in their brightness. How beautiful and precious the hope that in-shines through this window.—Think! "others toiling, striving, suffering as we, will catch from us in the days to come, some touch of tender, helpful comfort, if now, in the hour of trial, we hold fast to God and to holiness."

You remember, dear H——, we prefaced this our "open window" meditation by the emblem held in sunrise; let us now seal it with the emblem of sunset—a metaphor no less meaningful. Not a cloudless sunset, when the world is flooded with the shimmer of a pale uniform light, but one heralded by cloud heaped high on cloud, for it is then that each catch a sunbeam that reveals a special ray of glory, bringing out now one and then another "sun and cloud" tinting of rainbow radiance, till at last the earth as well as sky is aglow with brightness.

A meaningful type, I repeat, for thus it is with the sorrows and trials of life; through the shining on them of God's care for us, they each and every one become a separate beam, till at last before the full glory of His Love and Light they roll away and the "Windows of Heaven" open with no shadow between our upward gaze, and His down-shining brightness.

May "God be merciful unto us, and bless us, and thus show us the Light"—even the light of His countenance. And He will, if in faith we seek it, for Christ said—"I am the Light of the world." Walk, then, as a child of light, "in quietness and confidence wherein is strength."

"Almighty God, who showest to those that are in error the Light of Thy truth, ...

and who alone canst order the unruly wills and affections of sinful men, grant unto Thy people that they may love the things which Thou commandest, and desire that which Thou dost promise : that so among the manifold changes of this world, our hearts may surely There be fixed, where our true joys are to be found ; through Jesus Christ our Lord. Amen "

www.ingramcontent.com/pod-product-compliance
Lightning Source LLC
Chambersburg PA
CBHW031815220426
43662CB00007B/652